# Once Upon a Deal...
## *Vol. 2*

### More stories about life, work & negotiation

Horace McDonald

First published in Great Britain by Practical Inspiration Publishing, 2025

© Horace McDonald, 2025

The moral rights of the author have been asserted.

ISBN  9781788607667   (print)
      9781788607674   (epub)
      9781788607681   (Kindle)

All rights reserved. This book, or any portion thereof, may not be reproduced without the express written permission of the publisher.

Every effort has been made to trace copyright holders and to obtain their permission for the use of copyright material. The publisher apologises for any errors or omissions and would be grateful if notified of any corrections that should be incorporated in future reprints or editions of this book.

EU GPSR representative: LOGOS EUROPE, 9 rue Nicolas Poussin, LA ROCHELLE 17000, France Contact@logoseurope.eu

Want to bulk-buy copies of this book for your team and colleagues? We can customise the content and co-brand *Once Upon a Deal... Volume 2* to suit your business's needs.

Please email info@practicalinspiration.com for more details.

An invaluable guide to life – I just wish I'd read it 30 years ago.
**Jane Garvey – award winning broadcaster**

*Once Upon a Deal...* not only offers insightful, thought-provoking strategies and analysis, it also provides real world practical advice on how to navigate and succeed in the of the art of negotiation. Horace has managed to distil his vast experience into a simple but compelling read. A fantastic tool for all.
**Amadu Sowe – Senior Vice President, Paramount**

A lively and entertaining guide to the often-undervalued art of negotiation that is full of practical advice and tips on how to end up with the best possible deal.
**Jonathan Prynn – Associate Editor, Evening Standard**

# Contents

Preface .................................................................................. xiii

Chapter 1: Effective preparation ............................................. 1
    Penalty! ................................................................................. 2
    Negotiator Barbie: lessons from Mattel's iconic success ........ 5
    'It's the economy stupid' ........................................................ 6
    Shifting sands ........................................................................ 9
    Trick or treating .................................................................. 12
    Man 'o' man ........................................................................ 14
    Blossoming confusion ........................................................ 16
    Crystal balls ........................................................................ 18
    AI gone wrong… ................................................................. 20
    Giving to get ....................................................................... 22
    Olympic success ................................................................. 24
    Caught off guard? ............................................................... 27
    Please open the gate! ......................................................... 28
    No alarm and no surprises ................................................. 30
    Looking through my lens… ................................................ 32
    Unwrapping success in the retail industry ........................ 34
    The house always wins ...................................................... 36
    Do you say yes to the dress? .............................................. 38

Chapter 2: The Argue step ............ 41
   A stitch in time .......... 42
   The importance of being open .......... 43
   The not so subtle art of persuasion .......... 46
   Behaviour breeds behaviour .......... 48
   It's not you, it's me .......... 50
   Think fast, slowly .......... 52
   Sliding windows .......... 54
   Back off! .......... 56
   Negotiating space .......... 58
   The sooner the better… .......... 61
   Biden bows out .......... 64
   Hyperbole .......... 67
   Do you feel lucky? .......... 68
   Question mark .......... 70
   Power play .......... 72

Chapter 3: Reading and responding to signals .......... 75
   Get the picture? .......... 76
   A negotiator's crystal ball? .......... 78
   The sound of silence .......... 82
   Signal failure? .......... 85
   Not even in the room .......... 87
   'These are not the droids you are looking for' .......... 90
   The imbalance of power .......... 92
   Flash Keegan .......... 94

## Chapter 4: Creating momentum through proposals ......... 97

My kind of proposal this Valentine's ............................ 98
A Messi way to negotiate ............................................. 101
Brownie points ............................................................. 104
Go extreme or go home .............................................. 106
Rubbish on the streets of Edinburgh ......................... 109
Two important tactical negotiating lessons .............. 112
Tell me why… ............................................................... 115
Who goes first? ............................................................. 117
A strategy in need of surgery? .................................... 119
Proposals that take the risk ......................................... 121
The meaning of lie ....................................................... 123
Pholly ............................................................................. 125

## Chapter 5: Packaging to create more value ............. 129

It's a man's world? ........................................................ 130
When is the price the *price*? ..................................... 133
'Tis a season to be (not so) jolly .................................. 135
'Ave yer done? .............................................................. 137
You want it when???? .................................................. 140
Another fine mess! ....................................................... 141
The hair stays ................................................................ 143
Drastic discounts or deception… ............................... 145

## Chapter 6: Bargain to create more value ................. 147

Price increases .............................................................. 148
Cupid's arrows .............................................................. 151

Just plumb wrong! .................................................................. 153

Pennies from heaven? .............................................................. 156

The past is a foreign country: they do things differently there .................................................................. 159

Creativity: it's more than just chickens confronting existence .................................................................. 161

Red, red line .................................................................. 162

Beware the perils of giving in .................................................................. 165

From left field .................................................................. 166

The bank is closed… .................................................................. 168

Chapter 7: Close to getting the deal over the line ............. 171

Beware the trap of just one more thing .................................................................. 172

Do I or don't I say? .................................................................. 174

Chapter 8: Agree and document what has been agreed .................................................................. 177

What did I just agree to, again? .................................................................. 177

Mine all mine .................................................................. 179

When you let 'the boss' get involved in the negotiation when they are not prepared .................................................................. 182

Wanna bet? .................................................................. 183

Agreeing: the work of the devil .................................................................. 186

Once Upon a Deal… – Author bios .................................................. 189

John McMillan (Scotwork Founder) .................................................................. 189

Alan Smith .................................................................. 189

Stephen White .................................................................. 190

Horace McDonald ...... 190
David Bannister ...... 191
Tom Feinson ...... 191
Annabel Shorter ...... 192
Ellis Croft ...... 192
Ann Parr ...... 192
Siobhan Bermingham ...... 193

Index ...... 195

# PREFACE

Looking back over the 50 years since Scotwork began to run negotiating skills courses, it is interesting to note what has changed and what has not. The skills have not changed, nor the way that participants learn: by watching, doing and reading. These remain an integral part of our courses. Technology has continued to evolve and our audience has shifted, and the way clients do business has changed – but the ability of our consultants to observe the live negotiations and to offer constructive feedback and advice has not.

My involvement in negotiation began at university and continued in my first job as a sales engineer. I was involved in many negotiations but had never received any specific training in the process. When I formed Scotwork in 1975, initially to offer a different service, I began to pull together all that I understood about negotiating and to offer this as a skills training course. We were pioneers in the field. Video recording of the negotiations and replaying the results was ahead of its time. Many people had never heard themselves and most had never seen themselves before.

It never ceases to amaze me how universal the skills of negotiation are, and how 'The 8-Step Approach' applies across the different cultures of the 48 countries, including the UK, North and South America, Continental Europe and Asia, in which Scotwork is present.

Over the past 50 years we have watched thousands of negotiations and increased our understanding of the process:

what works, what doesn't; what produces a good outcome and what does not. We have continuously improved our course methodology, technology and content so that it can continue as the number one in terms of quality, effectiveness and global reach as we begin our next half century.

**John McMillan**

Founder & Chairman
Scotwork Ltd, Glasgow

# CHAPTER 1

# EFFECTIVE PREPARATION

Preparation is vital in negotiation; many would argue that it's the most important of The 8-Step Approach. The more complex the negotiation, the greater the need for preparation. However, this process needs to be gone through for even the most basic negotiations. To maximise its effectiveness, here is a checklist of the key components:

- What are my **objectives**? What do I want or need to achieve?
- What are my **must-haves**? The things you must get to do a deal – this requires rigour.
- What are my **intends**? What are the things that I realistically would like to have?
- What is my **strategy**? (often confused with objectives) How will I get there? Also, you need to consider alternative strategies.

- What is my **wish list**? What else can I ask for? Develop this list, ignoring any constraints.
- What is my **concession list**? What can I offer the other party to get my **wish list** items?

Give yourself sufficient time to go through this process, it will serve you well. It is also important to repeat the exercise, looking at the negotiation from the other party's perspective, essentially to walk in their shoes.

If you're working in a team, take the time beforehand to run this process together. It will *always* be time very well spent. You put yourself at a major disadvantage if you go into a negotiation unprepared, particularly if the other party has prepared, which should always be your going-in assumption, not to mention the advantage you get if the converse is true!

# Penalty!

## *David Bannister, 16th March 2023*

On the day I began to write this blog, I featured the BBC, specifically the fact that it had decided to disband the BBC Singers, a group that has been in existence for almost a hundred years and which is renowned for its choral excellence and its outreach and diversity activities. According to the BBC, this cancellation would increase its 'quality, agility and impact'. I, and many others, think exactly the opposite. I went on to contrast the cost of the 18-strong choir, which is a million pounds a year, with the BBC's stand-off with Gary Lineker, the former footballer and sports presenter who had been asked to step back from the football television programme that he leads every week after placing on social media a Tweet likening government policy towards illegal immigrants to that of Germany in the 1930s. The cost of Lineker's fees to the BBC is 35% more than the whole annual running cost of the choir. My intention had been to reflect on the issue of value and the fact that it would be possible, arithmetically at least, to retain the BBC Singers and pay a pundit £350,000 a year to present *Match of the Day* without any overall cost increase. A win/win perhaps.

However, despite my intentions to use these events as a subject for a blog, matters moved quickly on. By the weekend, all the BBC's sports presenters had lined up alongside Lineker and withdrawn their labour from programmes they would have presented, which were mostly cancelled or made unrecognisable in the case of *Match of the Day* that was a fifth of its normal length and entirely free of commentary. The BBC's Director-General flew back from a trip to the USA and by Monday had capitulated. Lineker was reinstated and made no apology for his Tweet. It was the Director-General who issued an apology.

What, as negotiators, do we take from this? First, events escalated quickly: Lineker's picket line of other millionaire football pundits rapidly shifted the power balance away from the BBC when they withdrew their labour and scuppered the weekend's sports schedules. Add to this, the fact that opinion polls were on Lineker's side because many saw this as an issue about freedom of speech.

Judging the power balance in a negotiation is crucial and many get it wrong because they frequently underestimate their leverage. In this case, however, the BBC, as the employer and a huge corporation, flexed its muscles only to discover that previously unnoticed powers – their own staff and the public at large – would rise up and make life impossible. Not correctly assessing and acknowledging the power of your counterparty can cause you serious challenges in a negotiation (although I think it fair to say that no one predicted the pundits taking home their collective bat if I can be allowed to mix my metaphors).

The real issue here, however, is the fallout from this misjudgement. Two consequences that are common when this happens to negotiators are evident: loss of face and precedent. The BBC has conceded an important principle that its employees and contractors may not give opinions on matters which impinge on party politics. The Director-General has been blindsided and looks to many people to have handled the issue precipitately and ineptly – faced with a revolt he did not predict, he backed down with seemingly little attempt to defend his own position. I predict that he will come under huge pressure internally and externally and may not even survive. Possibly more important is the matter of precedent – what do you learn as a BBC employee from this? You learn that the corporation is weak in the face of resistance and the broader that resistance is, the weaker the corporation's resolve seems to be. This particular weekend has probably changed the relationship between the BBC and its influential and powerful employees and contractors forever and not for the better if you are a member of the BBC's management.

I think that the appropriate phrase is 'own goal'.

# Negotiator Barbie: lessons from Mattel's iconic success

*Ann Parr, 17th August 2023*

Feeling rather late to the party, we have finally, as a family, booked tickets to see *Barbie* this weekend.

Breaking box office records, *Barbie* has grossed over $1bn in the three weeks since its release – equivalent to almost ten times its budget. When I was a child the doll I wanted was not Barbie but Sindy, its UK equivalent. Yet, while Sindy was essentially de-listed by 1997, Barbie has grown in strength. Undoubtedly, this is in large part due to Mattel's appetite to create more diverse and inclusive versions of the doll – today there are 176 different types of Barbie.

Even since its launch in 1959, Barbie was ahead of its time, with dolls who had careers that were rare or unavailable options to women of the day. Astronaut Barbie was launched in 1965, two years after the first woman Soviet cosmonaut Valentina Tereshkova travelled to space, although it would be another 19 years before the second female astronaut would follow. In 1972, Surgeon Barbie hit the shelves, and by 1992 she was running for president.

The career and business world for this pint-sized plastic fantastic was clearly an easy one to navigate but for real women, the commercial world can still, on occasion, face us with outdated attitudes and challenges as a result.

As negotiators, regardless of gender, we can learn lessons from the huge success of Barbie through the decades. There are three key things I believe Mattel has done brilliantly that has ensured their success. First, they kept focussing on the global objective of growing Barbie as a brand rather than simply producing a product. For negotiators, retaining clarity on the key objective allows us to take a step back and re-focus rather than getting entrenched in detail or sidelined and distracted.

The second thing Mattel did (and arguably the most successful) was that they were creative and agile in how they achieved their objective. A focussed objective is great but the more flexible we can be around how to achieve that objective the better. Mattel's diversification into 176 different types of Barbie kept her relevant and inclusive and ensured an appeal to all that moved with the times.

Finally, Mattel built collaborations and partnerships as it grew. Working cooperatively with others to ensure mutually beneficial outcomes and develop trust is crucial for negotiators in long-term commercial relationships.

So, this weekend, in the spirit of all that is pink, my real-life Ken, AKA Mr AP and I, along with our daughter, will be sporting pink, entering the Barbie world and hopefully having a thoroughly good time!

## 'It's the economy stupid'
*Horace McDonald, 20th October 2022*

The news in the UK has been dominated in recent weeks by seemingly disastrous economic policy decisions outlined in a mini-budget created by the newly elected Prime Minister, Liz Truss, and delivered by her Chancellor, Kwasi Kwarteng. I say seemingly disastrous as the reactions outlined below have led to the removal of both from the most senior roles in the government and resulted in the shortest tenures in living memory.

Liz Truss was elected by a selection process, which has seen some 160,000 Conservative Party members selecting a Prime Minister, where she came a dismal third in the first round of voting amongst Conservative MPs. Some commentators have drawn a line to connect the decline of the British Empire, Brexit and an associated desire for low taxes as factors that underpin how the UK now finds itself isolated from Europe and apparently thinking that it can work outside the strictures of the global economy.

I'm not an expert in history, so will focus my attention on what can we, as negotiators, learn from this debacle, which has demonstrated a lack of planning, foresight and engagement on a herculean scale.

### Lesson number 1: Your proposal should be credible and support the facts

The mini-budget of 23rd September 2022 included £45bn of underfunded tax cuts, which had a huge impact on the bond and gilts markets, a fall in the value of the pound and will inevitably lead to even higher interest rates at a time when these are under extreme pressure due to high inflation. Whilst there are many people who are in favour of low taxes and a small state, its timing could not have been worse and the impact has been catastrophic.

### Lesson number 2: Know who your stakeholders are, part 1

It is highly unlikely that the economic policies that appeal to 0.005% of the British electorate and get you the top job will stand the test of public opinion. James Carvill, when advising Bill Clinton in 1992, coined the phrase 'it's the economy stupid'. Whilst the now abandoned income rate tax decreases, support for fuel bills and other measures would have helped some households, these gains will be wiped and much of the alleged growth in the economy rendered unachievable by increases in interest rates and the direct impact on mortgages. I know someone who works at a senior level in a major international bank, who told me that their profitability has significantly improved due to higher interest rates.

### Lesson number 3: Know who your stakeholders are and 'it's the economy stupid', part 2

That an Oxford-educated Prime Minister (politics, philosophy and economics (PPE) nonetheless), who was once Chief Secretary to the Treasury, and a Cambridge-educated Chancellor with a PhD in economic history, could have read the market's reaction so poorly simply beggars belief. I could refer back to A begat B, B begat C… but that's not the point here. Whilst the 99.995% of us who didn't vote for this PM had little power in influencing the government's decision making, the market's response was swift and visceral with the (independent) Bank of England not far behind.

### Lesson number 4: Always probe the *basis* of the proposal

The fact that the mini-budget was at odds with both the markets and the electorate (in polling the majority of the electorate were in favour of increased public spending to support the NHS and the socially disadvantaged and not tax cuts) was bad enough.[1] But to expect that £45bn of underfunded tax cuts would not be challenged by every news and economic commentator and be savaged by the markets was naïve and suggests a poor understanding of context and economic reality.

**Lesson number 5: *Time* is a key variable**
To expect that the mini-budget would not be subject to scrutiny was bad enough. To expect to be able to wait two months before you explain to the Office of Budget Responsibility how the tax cuts would be funded seems nothing short of folly.

We learn from our mistakes, often these are forgivable. There comes a point though...

# Shifting sands
*Horace McDonald, 28th September 2023*

After 11 weeks, the football transfer window in England closed on Friday 1st September, so you might ask why I'm reporting on this a couple of weeks after; I'll come to that later. In England, the transfer circus dominates the sports media and Sky Sports News devotes hours of coverage with various experts and influencers speculating which player is joining which team and at what price. The window itself is 'manna from heaven' for Sky Sports, well it is if I'm a typical viewer. The output model is like that of a commercial pop radio station constantly repeating songs in that if you listen

---
[1] YouGov Poll.

for an extended period, it's the same players being talked about endlessly across the day.

In negotiation, one of the key variables, and perhaps the most important, is time management. Whilst not all the transfer windows contain the same level of drama and intrigue, there is a familiar pattern. The Premier League summer window ran from 14th June to 1st September, plenty of time for clubs to organise their transfer dealings you might think; however, it's not as simple as that. The global market is dominated by the big clubs and the English Premier League spent £2.36bn on new players, which accounted for 48% of the spending across the big five European leagues. It is not always the case that the biggest clubs spend the most money; however, they dominate the market for marquee players and the smaller clubs benefit from the inevitable release of players from the big clubs to the smaller clubs. Also, the lateness of these deals can result in a transfer not happening due to a lack of time available for a club to replace a player going to another club.

The big story of the 2023/24 summer window isn't the eye-watering amount of money spent by English clubs, but the emergence of the Saudi Pro League, who spent upwards of £800m by the UK deadline and whose presence came as something of a surprise to both the media and clubs themselves. Given the amount of investment by Saudi in several sports, indeed including owning and sponsoring some of the biggest clubs in Europe, it would be easy to assume that the major clubs should have seen this coming.

Previously, the Saudi's approach appeared not dissimilar to that of the US Major Soccer League (MLS) in that they focussed on proven talent at major clubs at the very end of their careers. However, not surprisingly, the game changer has not been money spent on transfers, but the eye-watering (tax-free) salaries available, sometimes three or four times the salaries of already very highly paid players. As an aside, I don't subscribe to the narrative that footballers are overpaid. In what is a short career, the politics notwithstanding, it's hard to argue when players can set themselves up for life during a two- to three-year stint, which has resulted in a very different profile of players moving East.

Arguably the club in the Premier League that has been most impacted by this new development has been Liverpool FC. Whilst their manager, Jurgen Klopp, had a plan to overhaul their ageing midfield, the emergence of the Saudi League transfer strategy made this a reality sooner than expected, with the loss of two of his key midfield players. But that wasn't the last of it, the Saudi window ended later than in the UK and Al-Ittihad came in with a last-minute bid of £150m for their most prized asset, Mohamed Salah, with a reported salary of £2.45m per week. Liverpool turned down the offer. However, the smart money suggests that Al-Ittihad will be back in the January window with an increased offer. As a Muslim, Salah will undoubtedly be seen as a huge coup for the Saudi League and I daresay that Liverpool is considering how they will invest the proceeds into new talent.

The big clubs are now run more like corporations, with CEOs, managers, Directors of Football and vast staffs to manage players' health and well-being. Much like in negotiation, strategy development is key, and managing and attracting the right talent is paramount. In any strategy development, it is important to consider as many options as possible and understand the external factors that will impact your strategy. From the outside, it appears many of the big clubs did not see the emergence of the Saudi League and were taken by surprise as a result. Easy in hindsight, I know, but given the portents and the fact that the world's most highly paid player (Cristiano Ronaldo) is plying his trade there, perhaps it shouldn't have been. Taking as broad a perspective as possible, looking at the market from the perspective of a competitor and understanding the assets at their disposal will always bear you in good stead.

# Trick or treating
*Siobhan Bermingham, 19th October 2023*

As the excitement and expectations of Halloween are building, I've been reflecting on the various negotiation strategies I implemented from a young age during Halloween. I remember the anticipation – as the youngest of six children, I'd watched my five brothers come back with huge buckets full of sweets. It was finally my turn! Although I couldn't go as far from home as they could, this was my chance – my first time trick or treating! Time was limited (much like it can be in negotiations), so I had to have a clear strategy. We focussed on the houses closest to home to maximise the chances of filling our buckets with treats that we could proudly show off to our eldest brothers.

My youngest brother and I set off full of pride in our Halloween costumes believing that people would be amazed at how good we looked and freely begin offloading the treats, much like the stories our eldest brothers had told us. We knocked on an elderly gentleman's door. We regularly waved to this neighbour so we were sure it would be a good house to start with. After we excitedly said 'trick or treat' we waited expectantly. No sweets… (no free concessions in this negotiation. We stood clutching our empty buckets hopefully). The neighbour asked us to perform our 'tricks' and reminded us that you don't get 'treats' for nothing in life. Needless to say, he was underwhelmed with us shouting 'boo' and jumping towards him. He told us to work on our tricks for next year and gave us one of the smallest sweets each from his big bowl.

We continued our trick or treating. Some gave fruit (to my mum's delight), others gave handfuls of sweets, and some specified just one sweet. Much like in negotiations, there are those that hand out several 'treats' as goodwill gestures and those that teach us we mustn't be greedy and will only get something if it's traded for (in this case, a decent Halloween 'trick'). The elderly gentleman we first visited certainly taught us that he will only trade a sweet on the condition of us performing a 'trick'. New strategy – prepare a decent 'trick' for him in advance. We upped our game, went back, and he rewarded our efforts with the largest chocolates in the basket.

Over the years, I noticed how there are some negotiators who added on 'goodwill gestures', free concessions that were unconditional. Rather unfortunately for them, this taught us to expect the 'treats' each time we came to the table to negotiate, rather than reciprocate with our own 'treats'.

In my commercial career, I remember when one particular partnering company had a significant budget cut and suddenly their generous goodwill gestures were gone – no more free treats. Everything was traded for. If we agreed to something they wanted, we'd get something that we wanted. Although the sudden change was uncomfortable initially, we certainly learned to shift our expectations and became more creative in our preparation, so we had lots of concessions we could trade to get things on our wish list. It certainly motivated us to be far more creative and strategic in our negotiations and ultimately resulted in far more fruitful contracts for both parties.

Which sort of negotiator are you? Do you find yourself handing out handfuls of 'treats' unconditionally and forgetting the value those items may hold for the other party? Or are you trading concessions to get something that you want from your wish list?

Preparation is key to creating strong wish and concession lists that you can trade with in a negotiation. Avoid being like my younger self, struggling to be creative under pressure – my shouting 'boo' and jumping certainly didn't hit the mark!

## Man 'o' man

### *Horace McDonald, 9th November 2023*

Lunch for me on most days is me walking into the house from the bottom of my garden and preparing a light meal, often an omelette, shared with my wife. I often turn on the TV to catch up on the sports news or watch a bit of sport, which now is mostly the Cricket World Cup. My partner loathes cricket but that doesn't compare to the level of invective aimed at the

TV when an ad for a 'shoot 'em up' video game appeared on the TV recently. Her searing claim 'that men start wars and when they're not fighting them, they're playing video games that mimic war' is hard to argue with.

Earlier today my Scotwork colleague Alan Smith mentioned in a WhatsApp that he'd stopped listening to the news; understandable. For many years my work day would start with being woken up to Radio 4, which has ceased since my commuting career finished in early 2019. However, with the war raging in parts of Europe and the Middle East, an enquiry looking at the calamitous picture being painted about the current UK government's management of the pandemic on top of all the other stuff makes news sometimes scary, but it has encouraged me to put my phone away and start listening again and it can only be Radio 4 (I am aware other news outlets are available).

Good news outlets understand that the news is one element, but good analysis is the key to build depth. Russia's invasion of Ukraine is over 600 days old and with any modern conflict attention dissipates over time. The news cycle is now dominated by Israel's response in Gaza to the attack by Hamas on 7th October. A recent Radio 4 interview featured Lord (Peter) Ricketts, who was on the Arab/Israel desk when Israel embarked on a not dissimilar foray into Lebanon around the formation of the PLO (Palestinian Liberation Organisation) in 1982 and later became the British Ambassador to France. He remarked that there are several similarities to 1982 with his central thesis that military operations (he didn't use the word war) don't achieve political objectives and will always come to an end. What is left is a vacuum of how the invaded territory will be governed when the operations end and the incentives that can be developed to give the people left behind a sense of a brighter future.

War, yes, let's use the term, can be described as the ultimate means of imposing your will on another country or territory to fulfil a certain objective, such as eliminating Hamas or returning Ukraine to a union with Russia. History tells us that the absence of realistic strategies once the initial objective has been met often results in years of further pain for the people left behind in a political vacuum and can also lead to greater security issues in the longer term. As negotiators this helps us understand the futility of unilateral action leading to a successful resolution to a conflict.

## Blossoming confusion
*Ellis Croft, 11th January 2024*

Over Christmas I was struck by the number of trees in full blossom around my neighbourhood in London – yes, the weather was very mild, but in mid-winter, it was still quite a surprise to see such a sign of spring so abundant.

This week, the return of two familiar things brought this back to mind: the cold snap we're currently embracing, or enduring depending on your point of view, and teaching my first course of 2024. On the first of those, the cold front rushing into the south of the UK reintroduced an almost comforting certainty about the time of year and what we ought to expect from it. Unmistakable, it's very cold indeed, so don't forget your scarf, hat and gloves. The second, observing teams negotiate the conflict situations we give them, was a timely reminder about how varied the ways in which what is definitive to one party can be interpreted entirely differently by the other. It struck me that while I was surprised by the blossom I noticed at Christmas – because it was late December and the arrival of blossom on trees usually heralds the warming effects of spring – all that the trees were doing was responding to the stimulus around them, which of course was the ambient temperature.

In a similar way, what we believe we are transmitting to our negotiating counterparts as clearly and simply as possible can sometimes result in the entirely unexpected. When I was working in magazine publishing some years back, one of the existential challenges of the job was managing decline, as the then-nascent digital media encroached upon print audiences with ever-increasing voracity. This required regular conversations with suppliers about ever-decreasing volumes and rarely involved good news. So, on one occasion where our team had hit upon a successful niche around supplements and special editions, I had the rare opportunity to talk with our printer about good news – wonderful! So I carefully planned how to introduce this incentive, wanting to use the leverage it gave us wisely. 'We're looking at the potential to publish special editions of the title and I've some ideas on what we'd target as a realistic cost for those,' I opened, expecting an enthusiastic and excited response to what I thought was a clear proposition. The bitter disappointment I faced from our printer was, therefore, a surprise. Much like the blossoming tree in December, it transpired that their response was based on the ambient temperature. Our printer, looking at the steady decline in circulation, had taken the statement not as good news of separate and additional business, but as confirming that we would be replacing the weekly publication with a monthly or even quarterly title instead.

I hadn't taken the temperature before sharing my news – doing so may have helped me reframe the proposition in a way that would have given me the leverage I sought. It's always in a negotiator's interests to be able to see the world through the eyes of those they are making deals with – take the time to ensure you can, and you're very likely to trade much more effectively.

## Crystal balls
*Ellis Croft, 1st February 2024*

At the start of the year, it's entirely normal to see all manner of predictions for the forthcoming year broadcast across just about any and every media we consume. Fair enough, many of us are curious and where's the harm in a bit of speculation? Take on board the fact that it's very likely to be an election year in the UK (and it most certainly is in the US) and this tendency to read the runes can become all-pervasive.

One of the main drivers of our fascination with these forecasts is, of course, the fact that they are endlessly debatable – they're dealing with future events, after all. Well, I say 'endlessly', but of course that highlights the trouble with predictions; at some point, their accuracy is determined by the passage of time, which of course does end the debate. The prediction either rewards or damns the prophet. If you're canny enough then you can cast your predictions far enough into the future that in the unlikely event you're right you'll be heralded as a visionary – and if you were wrong, few are likely to remember your error(s).

What if time were flexible, though? Then you might argue that your prediction is still valid and that it simply hasn't happened *yet* (fans of end of the world conspiracy, look away now). And indeed this is a common refrain among many soothsayers – their version of the future is still sound, it's just that the conditions that looked bang on last week to make it happen were actually static interference. The prediction is solid, it's everything else that's wobbling around it. If we wait, it will happen.

What does this have to do with negotiation? One of the critical skills underpinning good deal making is preparation, and in preparing to negotiate, we must address future conversations. We'll need to structure expectations, ask good questions and understand those we negotiate with in order to progress. In doing this it can become incredibly tempting to second-guess those with whom we negotiate – what they're likely to want, say, think, do, how they're likely to approach the deal and so on. The risk we run in doing so is that like our doomsday friends, we can end up waiting a very long time for what we imagined coming to pass. And for many of us, time is precious. Worse still, we run the risk that we will miss, ignore or dismiss information that would be incredibly useful simply because it doesn't conform to what we're expecting or looking for.

I wouldn't advise that you ruthlessly eliminate anticipating what the other party might want when preparing – far from it. Like predicting that a certain golf-playing serial defendant may secure the nomination for the Republican Party in the 2024 US election, much prediction is evidence-based and probable, and can therefore add value. When planning for the future, remember that probability is simply a useful indicator – and reality is a much more useful companion when you are negotiating.

## AI gone wrong...
### Siobhan Bermingham, 22nd February 2024

As Artificial Intelligence's (AI) presence in the commercial world increases, a recent Canadian tribunal has many questioning how reliable AI is when it comes to sales, negotiation and customer interaction.

AI is being utilised across industries to assist businesses in automating tasks, enhancing decision making with data analytics, personalising marketing campaigns, optimising supply chain logistics, predicting trends for strategic planning and improving customer service through chatbots.

Air Canada has been ordered to pay compensation to a customer who was informed by a chatbot that they could purchase a ticket and later claim a partial refund due to bereavement. There is much debate about who is responsible when chatbots get it wrong. Air Canada argued that the chatbot is a 'separate legal entity'. The court ruled that Air Canada must take responsibility for any refunds promised by the AI chatbots on their website.

Although the terms, timing and process in the refund claim are where the issues in this particular situation arose, it does raise the question of how reliable AI is when negotiating the finer details of a sale/contract. Who should be held responsible when AI gets it wrong and what measures are in place to ensure AI isn't misinforming customers or businesses?

As more and more companies begin to integrate AI technology into their front- and back-end processes, there must not only be an awareness of the value AI brings but also the rate at which it is changing. Companies will need to ensure their positioning and safeguarding against potential issues evolve at the speed of AI's development.

This brings us to more rampant debates at present – should AI be classed as a separate legal entity? Will we humans be able to keep track/be in control of AI? Will there come a time when we have to consider the sentience of AI? Will AI be held responsible for misinformation, and how will that put businesses in a position of strength or weakness over the coming years?...

When it comes to negotiating, AI now has decision support systems and data analysis abilities that can certainly help with preparation. Decision support systems can help you to analyse potential negotiation scenarios, create wish and concession lists or consider constraints that may affect the negotiation. All of these can be helpful in preparation for a negotiation when time is of the essence. Analysis by AI of large volumes of data, market trends, patterns and similar deals can also help with strategic preparation. So, we certainly aren't suggesting that AI hasn't got a place in negotiation – we merely need to understand how to best utilise it.

## Giving to get
*Ellis Croft, 27th June 2024*

Last week I got to see the excellent *Nye* at the National Theatre. Nye Bevan was a Minister for Health who spearheaded the creation of the British National Health Service (NHS).

The play covers a broad chunk of Bevan's life and career and does so with humour, pathos and no small amount of drama. It's a lot to squeeze into a 2hr 40 minute run time – possibly as a result of this, one of the most dramatic sequences flashes by with almost indecent haste. The scene I have in mind is the final approach of 5th July 1948 – the day on which the NHS replaces all that went before it in terms of the UK's healthcare.

Prior to the NHS, access to medicine across the UK was largely determined by the ability of patients to pay GPs or consultants. The other means of accessing healthcare was via charitable hospitals or, more recently, community health services, whereby the local population all paid in to cover the entire community (as pioneered in Tredegar in Wales by Bevan himself). It was clear that this patchwork quilt of differing standards, layers of access and concentration of resources was sub-optimal, particularly following the Second World War, which had seen a massive increase in how closely the state monitored public health, morale and more. The Beveridge Report, which paved the way for Bevan, specified that universal healthcare that was accessible to all would lead to dramatic improvements in the nation's collective health.

The run-up to the birth of the NHS did come with more conflict than might be imagined from our vantage point more than 70 years later – conflict that required some insight and action that is still utterly relevant to negotiators today. Strange as it may seem today, not only was the NHS bitterly opposed before its creation, but also the strongest opponents were led by the British Medical Association (BMA), effectively the trades union for Britain's GPs, doctors and consultants. A philosophical objection to the socialisation of a profession – Bevan's role as Health Minister was even sniped at as being 'Medical Fuhrer' as opponents sought to use recent memory to demonise the idea of the NHS – was accompanied by very pragmatic opposition to moving from a consulting/practice-based remuneration to being state employees. In other words, money. The BMA's opposition to the NHS was implacable and they had seen off previous Health Secretaries before Bevan. And yet Bevan got what he wanted; and this is where, as a negotiator, I'm fascinated by the story. What can we learn?

1. **Be clear on your objective**: Bevan wanted universal healthcare free at the point of service (a principle that still largely operates today). He got that. Which means that…
2. **Prepare to be flexible**: Recognising that many BMA members were opposed to the change in employment and remuneration structure, rather than the principle of universal access, Bevan's strategy was simple – make concessions that would get around this obstacle in pursuit of the actual objective itself. Leading to…
3. **Negotiation is the art by which we give in order to get**: The skill lies in making sure that what we give is of lesser value to us than what we get in return. Bevan's

concessions (GPs were allowed freedom to run their practices, consultants retained the ability to practise privately as well as through the NHS, and doctors and nurses were offered more by way of salary) enabled him to secure agreement, delivering what by any measure was and remains a worthwhile objective.

The broad lessons in objective setting – keeping a simple and flexible strategy and preparing in advance the variables with which you can trade to agreement – are as relevant today as they were in 1948. We might not be doing deals that lead to the kind of outcomes the UK has benefitted from in terms of the creation of the NHS, but they'll only ever be better deals when we remember those lessons.

## Olympic success

*Horace McDonald, 1st August 2024*

The statistics state that over a billion people will have watched the Paris 2024 Olympic opening ceremony last Friday. It was certainly one to remember, what with the rain and the extent to which it sought to represent diversity in all its forms throughout. I'm not sure I'd spend four hours watching it again but it surely was a spectacle to be remembered.

The number of sports represented at the event has grown to such an extent that the BBC (and I suspect every terrestrial broadcaster) can no longer cover all of them. This is in stark contrast to London 2012 when my then 12-year-old son spent two weeks on the sofa watching all sorts of arcane sports with his mum and loved every minute. We were also fortunate enough to have acquired tickets for one of the days of the athletics. My son moved back home last weekend, costing me a small sum, as I've had to pay to access certain sports, in this case basketball.

My wife and I went to a gig the night he moved back in and we got home late in the evening to see our son watching a documentary about the British sprinter Linford Christie. I mentioned that I'd been told that the one featuring Daley Thompson (Olympic Decathlon Gold Medal Winner in 1980 and 1984) had come highly recommended and despite the fact that my wife and I had to leave for France for an early morning flight, we then watched the majority of that programme. This brought back a ton of memories as well as some unique insight into the man himself; from him and some of the people who knew him well. Undeniably, one of the most talented and dedicated athletes ever to emerge from the UK.

In recent Olympics by any comparative measure (GDP per capita, indexed population), the UK has performed extremely well by way of its medal haul. Much of this has been made possible by the contribution from the National Lottery. Since their funding for Olympic and Paralympic sport started, British athletes have won 863 medals, the majority of which have gone to rowing and cycling. By contrast, Thompson received next to no money to fund his training. Things were certainly different in the 1970s and 1980s.

On a personal level, the Olympics come alive when the athletics starts. Daley's career coincided with the very intense rivalry between two very talented middle-distance runners: Sebastian Coe (who features in the documentary) and Steve

Ovett. To say that the relationship between the two runners was less than cordial is an understatement. With the later emergence of Steve Cram, the UK dominated 800m and 1,500m events for many years and the end of their careers left a gap that the UK has found difficult to fill. However, the emergence of Jake Wightman and Josh Kerr who have won the last two World Championships at 1,500m puts the UK firmly back in the running.

Whilst many people enjoy the drama of the sprints, the 800m and 1,500m events are the most interesting as they are the races where arguably planning is paramount. All of the athletes at this level will have a clear understanding of their *objectives*. Although all the competitors in the final hope to win the race, it will be a select few who can realistically win a medal and some of the runners will see making the Olympic final as a huge achievement, which it undoubtedly is. Similarly, the athletes and their teams will have collected a significant amount of *information* about all of the competitors in the field and will be using this to plan how each of their athletes will manage their races.

The most intriguing element for me is the need for a flexible *strategy*. Whilst the 5,000m and 10,000m races are interesting, the need for the level of strategy required only really comes into play in the last two to three laps. In the 800m and 1,500m, this need for think, plan and execute in the race is constant and these races for me are the most exciting.

Yes, each athlete will have a dominant strategy, linked to their abilities and often linked to their finishing speeds compared to the other athletes, but these will need to be constantly updated and renewed as the races unfold. I'm expecting it to be a very exciting week.

## Caught off guard?
*Annabel Shorter, 2nd March 2023*

Way back in my early career as a Castrol retail sales representative, I bowled into an account in Dorchester to wow my customer with my latest promotion on Castrol GTX. Ten minutes later I left, holding back tears and biting my lip.

It would seem that the owner was less than impressed with the level of discount I had offered, or certainly the way that I had explained it. He shouted, he bawled, bits of spit flew from his mouth and his eyes blazed. Such was the level of vitriol aimed at me.

The following day I drove back the 50 miles, walked back in again, and explained it again. I left with the order and an apology. Interestingly, it seemed I had received the brunt of his frustration about a number of issues that day.

That was about 30 years ago, and I remember it vividly. Fundamentally, I had returned as I wanted to ensure that I knew how to handle the situation and not become intimidated or dissuaded by this. It's not easy.

These days I am a lot older (and I hope a little bit wiser) and I have 15 years of experience training, teaching and consulting for Scotwork, but I don't mind admitting that a few years ago I was treated in a similar way, and it still caught me off guard.

A seemingly decent gentleman greeted a colleague and me in the reception area of his company. He chatted convivially as we made our way to the informal chat about how we might help their business. We had been asked to have this meeting with one or two members of the commercial team.

We entered the room to be greeted by about a dozen stony-faced people, sitting in a horseshoe, facing the two chairs placed front and centre, which were to be the focus of the interrogation. Suffice to say, we left an hour later, fuming with anger but battered, bruised and belittled. More than anything, I was determined never to find myself unprepared again for such a situation. It was a timely reminder of the very real pressures and behaviours that negotiators face.

# Please open the gate!
## *Ellis Croft, 19th January 2023*

Alumni of our courses may sense something familiar about the photo accompanying this blog – a group of sheep, standing forlornly at a shut gate, unable to progress along their chosen path (let's for a moment ignore the sheep on the right who appears to be considering their options).

It's an example of how obstacles can become impassable – even when they're not. Negotiators need to be keenly aware of such obstacles, recognising them first before assessing alternative choices.

I was sent this photo by a former colleague (a fellow alumnus) who knew it would tickle me, given what I do now. Indeed it did, and so much so that I thought it would be an entirely appropriate platform on which to base a blog for the new year. Blogging is one of the pleasures of the job, particularly when the muse is in, and with such a perfect photo what could go wrong? And so I set about my writing with all the gusto you might expect with a fresh new year's breeze in my resolute sails. So many examples to choose from! Decades of experience in media gave me a veritable Aladdin's cave of gates from which to choose; my own experiences of selling, managing teams, purchasing and internal negotiations also produced a plethora of participants in the last year alone that had shared stories of their own organisational gates. And could I capture any of this in the way I wanted to? Bah! No, I could not.

I had composed around a dozen or so different blogs, all of which I'd rejected or was otherwise unhappy with. By now, the deadline was starting to loom and a pleasurable and insightful experience of writing a blog was starting to take on something altogether different and less enjoyable. It took me so many attempts that it was only after I worked on a course last week – and hence had an enforced break from the cursed photo – that I realised. In writing about sheep at a gate and stretching every metaphor beyond breaking point, I'd constructed, walked to and stubbornly bashed my head against a self-made gate. My objective was to write a blog. The inspiration for that blog was simply one method by which to facilitate my objective – but instead, it had become an obstacle. And once I recognised that, it wasn't too hard to walk around the gate.

Do your best to avoid gates!

## No alarm and no surprises
*Horace McDonald, 7th December 2023*

Negotiations are made up of several issues/variables, most of which have a different value to each party. We define negotiation as a process by which parties in conflict adjust their positions, by trading issues of lesser importance in exchange for issues of greater importance, because the agreement must be implemented by all parties. At Scotwork we ask participants in their planning to differentiate their issues between what we call their 'must-haves' and 'intends'. The former are effectively deal breakers. For illustration, if in the deal the minimum you can live with is a two-year contract, any deal that ends up at less than two years means that the deal cannot be done. Whereas, if you have greater flexibility on the contract length then you could be in a position to accept less than two years on the basis that you would use items from your wish list to ameliorate this reduction, for example, give them what they want on terms that are acceptable to you.

I was thinking about this having celebrated a very significant birthday two weekends ago. It was a bit of an up and down day as it started with huge joy as I was sent videos from two Crystal Palace players wishing me a happy birthday. My team then proceeding to lose to Luton Town for whom it was their first home win of the season. The day culminated in a rather wonderful party attended by over 100 guests.

Having sorted the venue, the food and drinks and the music, the next issue was how to manage the presents situation. I am a difficult person to buy for. We also advise that in a negotiation you are clear on what you want and on your non-negotiables, and I wanted to ensure that I didn't receive presents I neither wanted nor needed (in this case booze and books. I'm a Kindle person). Thus, I sent out specific instructions to the invitees. Not surprisingly, much as negotiations rarely go as originally planned, my instructions were not followed to the letter. I got some booze and a couple of books, but for the most part, my guests used their imaginations to great effect and I was given a number of great presents of things I neither thought I needed nor wanted but are still delightful. A few people took the easier option and bought me (as advised by my wife) gift vouchers from a rather splendid department store.

Having vowed not to go back to physical music and having thrown away all my vinyl and CDs many years ago, I've committed yet another volte-face and have used the vouchers to purchase a rather expensive turntable (thankfully I don't need any other equipment) and am starting a process of buying albums and know I'll get some for Christmas. The biggest beneficiaries in this change of heart are my children, as they now have more present buying options for me.

The title of this piece is a lyric from a Radiohead song. Similarly, The Rolling Stones sang 'You Can't Always Get

What You Want', but if you set your stall out early, you can mitigate and reduce the things you don't want by providing the right information, painful though that can appear…

## Looking through my lens…
*Siobhan Bermingham, 19th September 2024*

A big meeting was coming up, one that I'd been working towards for a year. I felt pretty confident I'd done my due diligence and established a track record of being reliable and trustworthy as far as I could tell. So, it's safe to say I was feeling as confident as I could be going into this negotiation but still I knew I had to take the time to thoroughly prepare. The other stakeholders were all about detail. They liked every 't' crossed and every 'i' dotted. They liked to know that I knew the project inside out, back to front and sideways. So I set to work thoroughly preparing, readying myself for the questions that might come my way. Drawing in any information, customer data and with KPIs (key performance indicators) almost coming out my ear holes, it's safe to say I'd prepared like never before. I'd even remembered to work on an opening statement outlining our expectations for a new five-year deal, significant growth and on and on…

I left my prep for a day, deciding that I needed a bit of head space so I could review it again before the meeting with fresh eyes to see if there was anything I'd missed. Coming back to it the morning of the meeting it seemed like I'd remembered and covered everything needed. I'd prepared,

I felt confident, this meeting might even be enjoyable… so off I went…

How wrong I was. Although I had prepared thoroughly, which enabled me to feel more in control and confident in the meeting, and I certainly had credible facts and reason behind the proposal I put on the table, I'd completely forgotten a crucial aspect of the preparation process. Assumptions!

I had filled all my preparation time with the information and data that related to my objectives and not at all taken the time to consider what assumptions I was making about the other party. As the meeting progressed it became very clear that my proposal, based on a five-year deal with significant increase in volume, was completely out of alignment with the lifespan of this project as far as they saw it. They were seeing this partnership through a completely different lens. This was a short-term project from their perspective and was introduced to initiate some fresher and newer ideas for their relaunch. They had no intention of continuing to use any of these products and had only done it as a temporary promotion. It all got rather awkward as I'd come in with such a strong pitch that they felt very uncomfortable in the process of setting me straight. Saving face in that moment was quite difficult and only half achieved.

From that moment on, it is safe to say that I always take the time to check with myself what assumptions I am making in my preparation and ensure that I test those assumptions in my meetings. An awkward experience that certainly reminds me to consider the deal through the other party's lens, not just my own.

# Unwrapping success in the retail industry

*Siobhan Bermingham, 14th December 2023*

'Tis the season for festivities, gifts and rampant retail sales. As the Christmas season is upon us, now is the time for the retail industry to transform products into bundles of Christmas joy. The skilful negotiators know this is a time of great success or great loss. Coordinating the supply, demands and sale of the 'must-have' items presents opportunities like no other season. Being able to understand the wants and needs of customers and negotiate lucrative deals with suppliers that prioritise those must-have items is key.

Retailers who want to sleigh (note the play on words there) this season, not only focus on discounts but also create magical experiences in their stores, reward customers for their loyalty (further developing their relationships) and create product bundles full of joy to set themselves apart from competitors instead. Negotiating this season of opportunity is far beyond pricing. Instead, it is important to understand what your customers value most and finding ways to deliver these at as low cost as possible. Magical Santa corners, elves, reindeer and decorations that make children squeal, all contribute to parents' favouring one store over another. Delivering dream items in a desirable way that is low cost to retailers can make a huge difference to sales and customer satisfaction. Displays that encapsulate the wonder of Christmas adorned with those must-get gadgets and beautiful clothing – the packaging and presentation of products are of greater importance now than any other time of year.

Customer service becomes far more crucial – discussing a customer's needs, priorities and those dream bonus/wish list items are key to helping sales teams bundle together packages as good as how Santa and his elves do it. Understanding those wish list items and having package deals available can grow one-off transactions into a sleigh full of purchases. If you want to negotiate greater profits, think of package deals rather than drastic discounts. Above all, keeping ahead of stock demands and building strong relationships with suppliers to assist in obtaining that unexpectedly popular, sometimes obscure, toy favourite of that season can ensure no child fears they've been added to the naughty list this Christmas – and potentially a life-long loyalty from a desperate present-hunting parent.

The twelve days of Christmas in the retail industry are a symphony of strategic implementation. Much like the classic song, it is filled with gifts of increasing volume; customers frantically shop with ever-increasing lists of food, decorations, presents, games to play and various other household needs that Christmas demands keep adding. Much like an orchestra, the Christmas retail period must be played with precision – adjusting accordingly to volume demands whilst negotiating skilfully with suppliers to be able to offer customers discounts but maintain retailers' profit margins and the ever-flowing supply of stock. A harmonious balance that must be led with maestro precision. The ominous fear of a bum note this season, echoing into 2024, is a price too high to pay for poor preparation.

As we wrap up another year, successful retailers understand that maximising this season of opportunity requires negotiating skilfully with suppliers, finding ways to bring greater value to their customers and delivering the feeling of Christmas magic, enabling retailers to unwrap maximum potential from the Christmas season.

## The house always wins
*Horace McDonald, 18th January 2024*

At the end of my road is one that connects two semi-major routes running west from Shepherd's Bush Green. We moved into this house almost 22 years ago to the day and, like many parts of London, the area represents an interesting bellwether of the national and local economy. At the time we moved in, the shopping at the abovementioned road was bookended by a small petrol station, which soon closed and became a car wash run by some very friendly Albanians (who cleaned my car for free), a number of unedifying pubs and two betting shops (you get the picture). Around 12 years ago, a notice was presented in another of the then-empty shops that an application had been made for another betting shop, which was thankfully rejected. Believe me, it's rather different now, we even have a Gail's (a store synonymous with wealth of an area)!

I rarely bet, but many people in the UK do. My gambling is limited mostly to the National Lottery, which I do very rarely. The Gambling Commission's latest report states that 22.5m adults gambled in the UK in 2021, which is reduced to

15.1m (40% of adults) if you exclude only those people who play the Lottery, and this spending has delivered total revenues of £14.1bn. Technology has played a significant role in the growing availability and complexity of the market, which has clearly brought a large number of people into it. On the downside, the number of problem gamblers has increased, as it no doubt becomes more difficult to stop when the next betting opportunity is available 24/7.

The difference between betting and negotiation is that in gambling, the odds are almost always stacked against you, as you're betting in an environment where you have little control and no amount of research will ever enable you to have more insight than the bookmaker, who manages the odds. Whereas in negotiation, effective preparation, constructive dialogue and realistic proposals are the key to success and provided you have some power, you stand a good chance of a successful outcome. Although have you ever tried negotiating with a bookmaker? They even take umbrage in a casino if you're seen to be counting cards.

This week sees the return of Brentford FC's Ivan Toney, who was found guilty of 262 breaches of the Football Association's betting laws in May 2023 and banned for eight months. It's undeniable that Toney would have known the rules; however, the number of bets that can now be placed on nearly every element of football can create a chimera of protection and technology will have paid a huge part in providing both the means and the evidence of Toney's access and subsequent penalty. Brentford are currently in a rut and will be stronger for his return.

On a more personal level, while Christmas memory is still relatively fresh, I am reminded of the one bet that got away. Working in the music industry, at the start of December one of the biggest topics of conversation was which song was going to be the Christmas No. 1. In the mid-1990s, our singles guru had evidence from the market that a song called 'Chocolate Salty Balls' from the US cartoon comedy *South Park* was building momentum in the market and had a shot. I placed a small bet (I think my colleague did as well because he loved betting on the horses) at 20/1 and the damned thing ended up at No. 2 behind the Spice Girls' 'Two Become One'. Only one of these songs has stood the test of time – however, both songs are unlistenable to me for very different reasons!

## Do you say yes to the dress?
*Andy Archibald, 2nd May 2024*

This week marks the beginning of May and the unofficial start to this year's wedding season.

Like many couples, my partner and I are getting married this year and have been busy planning the big day, including negotiating with multiple suppliers for everything from the venue to the cake. I'm sure most, if not all, brides out there will agree that finding the right dress is one of, if not the most, important things that need to be done. After getting engaged last year and deciding on the date and venue, up next for my partner was finding the right dress with the help of a bridal stylist. It was a (mostly) joyful experience shared with family and close friends. When confident that at last the dream dress had been found, the bridal stylist asked, 'Do you say yes to the dress?'.

For me, that is an exceptional question. In negotiation terms, the bridal stylist followed the eight steps of the process that's there in every negotiation. The **Preparation** was done beforehand by asking my partner to complete a survey and gathering initial *information*, including timescales. Further information was acquired by meeting at the shop and asking good questions to understand her dream wedding dress and budget, which we call the **Argue** step. A **Proposal** was made by suggesting a dress to try on, followed by numerous other dresses because either they were the wrong shape or were beyond the maximum budget. We call this the **Package** and **Bargain** steps of the process. However, once it was clear that there was a preferred dress and it ticked all the boxes, with the bridal stylist picking up on **Signals**, the bridal stylist asked for a response to their most recent **Proposal** and confirmed the other important details, which in negotiation terms is the **Close** and **Agree** steps of the process.

As trainers and consultants in negotiation skills, we recommend many things, including using the eight steps to take control of negotiations and, in most cases, making the first proposal in a negotiation. Provided the proposal is realistic, credible and addresses the needs of the parties involved, which can be identified by asking good questions in the **Argue** step, making the first proposal has numerous benefits, including putting the proposal maker in control of the negotiation. More often than not, first proposals are rejected by the other party, so be ready to hear 'no' and know that it's not the end. Ask why it's a 'no' and what it would take for the other party to agree. And always, always invite a response to your proposal – find your version of 'do you say yes to the dress?'.

# CHAPTER 2

# THE ARGUE STEP

This step is about information sharing and curiosity. Think of it as barristers putting forward their case (argument) in court, where they seek to ensure that the other side has a thorough understanding of their position, which is then reciprocated by the opposing counsel.

Done well, it is where both parties can build trust and develop a new or enhance an existing relationship. It provides each party with the opportunity to outline a clear view on their objectives, how they see the negotiation process progressing, while also enabling them to get a similar reciprocal picture from the other side. The **Preparation** stage will have developed a need to get a greater understanding of the other party's position and this step also provides the other party with the need to get a perspective on your position using well-thought-out questions. There are three key stages of the **Argue** step:

1. **The Opening Statement**: A rehearsed statement made at the beginning of the negotiation that provides the other side a clear view of your position and objective.
2. **Effective questioning**: To test your view of the assumptions you've made about the other party's objectives, thinking and position.
3. **Effective listening**: Hearing what they say, making notes, summarising to ensure understanding and developing more questions to maximise understanding.

# A stitch in time
## *Tom Feinson, 2nd February 2023*

'So, no swimming or football for the rest of your holiday.' These are the words my seven-year-old was desperate not to hear – but sadly he did. We were lucky enough to catch some winter sun at the end of 2022. My son was unlucky enough to cut his leg in the hotel grounds badly enough to need stitches (yes, there will be a claim, probably the subject of a subsequent blog) and those were the words of the doctor that stitched him up. He was not happy.

His unhappiness turned into outrage the following day when he saw one of his newfound holiday buddies heading to the football pitch. I overheard him demanding to my wife that he should be allowed to go and play. My wife, a lawyer, very calmly explained why he couldn't play. 'If your cut gets hit by the ball it will open again and be even worse.' He responded by saying that he kicked the ball with his foot not his leg and it would be fine. The argument escalated quickly, tension rose along with voices and tears flowed. I felt obliged to get involved and sadly only made matters worse. It was by now a full-blown row, with every reason given for not playing immediately unpicked, rejected and replaced with his justification for playing. I decided to impose my will. 'I understand your argument but you're not playing and that's the end of it.' Sadly, he did not accept this and continued to argue his case ignoring my repeated assertion that it wasn't happening. Twenty minutes of circular argument later, we were all emotionally drained and frustrated but my son was showing no signs of giving up the fight.

Then, in a moment of inspiration, I asked, 'What would it take for you not to play?'. To my surprise everything went quiet: the crying stopped, time stood still, a smile spread across his face and he said, 'A phone.'

I was impressed by the power of this simple question to reframe his mindset. I now had the challenge of meeting his demand but, in my view, that is a more constructive place to be than having a row. We agreed that when we got back to the UK he would be allowed to have one of my old mobile phones. 'Oh, and one more thing,' he said. 'I will get a SIM card, won't I?'....

## The importance of being open
*Horace McDonald, 13th April 2023*

On Good Friday my wife and I spent most of the afternoon into the late evening hanging out in central London with friends over dinner and a few too many drinks. One was a retired former work colleague (FWC) who I'd met very early in my career and our relationship developed over a mutual love of sport, including some very competitive matches on a squash court. Yes, it was that long ago!

My friend spoke about a pivotal moment in his career. As a young National Account Manager, he was given a big customer to manage, who had experienced significant grown through acquisition. The head of buying had a fearsome reputation in the industry and took great delight in devouring cowering account managers, particularly new ones. My friend's first meeting with his new nemesis carried even greater importance. This was well before the days when modern technology enabled retailers to manage stock in real time and, as many of their products were geared towards Christmas, orders needed to be placed at a key point in time to secure stock on shelves through the key period. The customer's Christmas order was important in my FWC's company for meeting its annual target, and my FWC had set a rather daunting objective of securing an order of £500,000, the equivalent of around £1.5m in today's money.

My FWC spent days figuring out his approach and undertook exhaustive preparation, taking as much counsel from his colleagues and his superiors as he could, but he knew that he would be held responsible for the outcome and its impact on him and his organisation. On the day itself, his nemesis played the typical tricks, including leaving him waiting in reception for 45 minutes without any offer of refreshment.

One of the challenges I see participants have when I'm in the classroom with them is the decisions they make about sharing information. Our advice is that you share information that supports your position and withhold information that does the opposite. Of course, not everything is quite as simple and, to a degree, this will depend on the nature of the relationship and the level of trust. My FWC recounted that at the start of the meeting he reached into his pilot case (remember them) as his instinct was to access his carefully prepared papers and, for reasons he couldn't explain, he realised that this was not the right course of action and instead decided to open the meeting by telling the buyer what he was in the room to achieve. At which point, the buyer left the room (for reasons my friend didn't understand) and they then spent three hours working on the deal, and my friend left the room with an order value of around £750,000! When asked why he'd been so helpful, the buyer said that he sees countless customers who talk too much, without purpose, who rarely articulate what they are trying to achieve. It turned out that he'd left the room to tell his PA to cancel his appointments for the rest of the day.

At Scotwork we call this the **Opening Statement** and its power is that it helps define your position and reveal any information that is critical to you achieving your objectives. Our view is that if you have bad news, or information that has a significant bearing on the outcome, it's best to reveal it early. My FWC had been on a Scotwork negotiation skills training course a couple of years earlier.

My FWC managed this challenging account for many years and the relationship was always conducted in a constructive manner, largely due to how their relationship started. So, don't be afraid to get your bad news on the table early. If the other party does choose to use it against you, at least you'll have learned something and if they don't, you'll have the potential to score a real advantage.

## The not so subtle art of persuasion
*Ellis Croft, 20th July 2023*

Three-word slogans: *Labour isn't working. Britain deserves better. Education, education, education. Take back control. Get Brexit done. Make America Great. Stop the boats.* I hate them. With a passion. Such meaningless drivel! Distilled to pointlessness. Why are they so popular?

Numerous treatises will have been composed on the effectiveness of these fun-sized manifestos down the years, but the aim of all of those cursed phrases? To influence, to persuade, to drive a point of view that will lead to a desired action (in all of the above cases, of course, that desired action being a vote for one or other political party). Certainly, persuasion is only one means by which we try and get what we want – there are other options. In politics some of them carry risk. Imposing your will generally looks a bit off in a democracy, although the flirtation with Erdogan/Orban style 'strong man' decision making has become something of a thing for politicians around the world, even where they are subject to the whims of the electorate. Postponement is a frequent visitor to many corridors of power, as the costs of those lovely promises become clearer and the long grass over there looks like a far better place for various policies. Giving in – whilst politically sometimes the most sensible option – does tend to attract the wrong kind of attention as accusations of U-turns fly. Problem-solving – arguably the primary function of a political executive – appears to have all but become extinct, with cross-party (or bi-partisan) initiatives looking deeply unfashionable in the face of the culture wars. Similarly, negotiation falls into this political classification – nobody seems keen to do the giving in order to get a bit, which of course underpins the trading that defines negotiation. We only have to look at the confused manner in which the US recently avoided debt default to see how afraid politicians are of negotiating, even where it's clearly in their own – and everybody else's – interests.

So we're back with selling or persuading to get what we want, at least politically. And in the same way that it doesn't help outcomes a great deal in policy terms, persuasion can be a dangerous enemy to the negotiator. Most of us will be familiar with the desire to come out on top of an argument – it's human nature, after all. But one of my favourite things about negotiation is that it frees us from the obligation to insist the other party agrees with our point of view. Removing these shackles is liberating – I no longer need to prove my point or wear down my opponent with three word slogans. Instead, I can focus on more valuable things such as listening to them, understanding their objectives and asking under what circumstances might a workable deal be realised between us. If I can then trade towards that, I can be entirely comfortable with the fact that they may fundamentally disagree with my position – if there's enough value in the deal for the both of us, that's by the by. Recognising the point at which persuasion ceases to be effective and starts to become counterproductive is a vital skill for any negotiator to hone. This brings us back to the ceaseless Punch-and-Judy ultra competitive show we see in many political arenas, where winning the argument is all. The limits of persuasion are routinely ignored and at a cost to all of us, in my view.

So, for negotiators. The best part? No more slogans. They mostly divide. Harm our interests. Increase mutual antagonism. Try listening, instead.

## Behaviour breeds behaviour
*Tom Feinson, 29th August 2024*

Anyone involved in negotiation will say that it's important to understand the wants, needs and motives of the other party. Phrases such as 'walk a mile in their shoes', 'seek first to understand before being understood' or 'negotiate from inside their head' are commonplace sayings. As an aside, I'm always cautious of that last phrase as it could be interpreted as manipulation. But back to the story… Of course, this is easier said than done – walking a mile in the shoes of that oily salesman, aggressive buyer, rude union official or intransigent manager can be uncomfortable, and those wise words begin to sound like glib aphorisms. So just imagine how hard it would be if the other party literally wants to burn down your house!

Recently, I watched a quite remarkable interview with Dr Abdul Hamid and Adam Kelwick of the Abdullah Quilliam Mosque in Liverpool about the approach they took when the police warned them that an angry mob were going to protest at their mosque that evening. The natural thing to do would be to batten down the hatches, make safe as much as you can, send staff home, or even worse, raise your own angry mob to shout down their angry mob.

They took a different approach; let me give some background. William Henry Quilliam, a solicitor from Liverpool, converted to Islam in 1887 after visiting Morrocco. He subsequently took the name Abdullah Quilliam – and the Abdullah Quilliam Mosque was founded in the same year and is the oldest in the country. Over 120 years ago rioters came to the mosque to protest, throwing stones and breaking windows (Islamophobia is not new). His response was to open the doors and invite people in to talk; they decided to follow his lead. The staff of the mosque cooked 200 burgers with chips and went out to the protesters and smiled, shared food, talked and listened. There was a lot they wanted to get off their chest – much of it was driven by a fear of the unknown and misinformation from third parties. Once they realised that many of the societal problems they were facing were mutual the mood changed. By the end they were hugging, shaking hands, exchanging numbers and organising to come back to the mosque to learn more.

This is a compelling and inspiring example of how conflict doesn't have to be confrontational. From a negotiator's perspective, it's much more constructive to unite than polarise, but that does take a genuine commitment to seeing the world from their perspective, which these guys did brilliantly. So, next time you think the other party is being unreasonable or rude rather than replying in kind, which is likely to escalate the conflict, it may be worth checking whether there is anything in what you are doing that has triggered it. Behaviour breeds behaviour; the behaviour you adopt will impact on their behaviour. Choosing constructive behaviour will help you achieve mutually beneficial results. As Adam said, in Islamic tradition 'a strong person is able to subdue anger even when it's justified.'

## It's not you, it's me
*Ellis Croft, 23rd March 2023*

A perennial topic of fascination for negotiators is the question of style – put simply, the manner in which we negotiate. Broadly speaking there are two behavioural approaches: competitive and collaborative. They can be influenced by all sorts of factors, such as context, innate preference, learned behaviours, mirroring, the power balance in the relationship – the list goes on.

### Collaborative

Many negotiators will readily agree that their commercial interests are best served by being collaborative. After all, if we want a long and productive relationship with a supplier or customer, leaving them feeling that they've lost out or been out-manoeuvred seems at best a counter-intuitive proposition. At worst, they'll be waiting by the school gates to get us back. With their bigger brother. Who bought fireworks on the school trip to France. And nobody wants that.

If we want to be collaborative, recognising the longer-term interests we represent, then thinking about the behaviours that influence our negotiating style is sensible. Being open breeds trust, which is valuable. Being comfortable with the other party's opinions – even where you disagree – is likely to keep the tension lower, again scoring useful points in terms of fostering collaborative partnership. An ability to rise above the fray and remain emotionally detached will aid our ability to navigate a course through a complex negotiation – and if both parties can achieve this, cooperative behaviour is certainly more likely an outcome.

## Competitive

Recognising these behaviours is one thing, of course, but pinning down where the behaviour that can drive competitive behaviour originates can prove more of a challenge, however. After all, behaviour tends to breed behaviour. I spent more than 20 years negotiating commercially, all the while telling myself that it was the other side of the table driving adversarial behaviour. I was convinced (quite bizarrely, as my partner will attest) that I was collaborative to the point of being conflict-averse. And then, a few short years ago, I took a personality profiling test specifically designed for business use. The questions were a doddle. Going through the outputs of that, the facilitator working with me commented (very mildly) that my results suggested that I was a good deal more conflict hungry than the average respondent. Well, with no small amount of relish, I rolled up my sleeves and launched into a shock-and-awe assault on the absurdity of such an outrageous calumny. About four or five minutes into my diatribe, the penny dropped.

Of course, many of us enjoy higher levels of self-awareness than I did – and that's good. Equally, recognising that there may be occasions where we are driving the behaviours we're holding the other party responsible for can be a valuable insight into taking concrete action to move our negotiations forward. I for one am happy to report that my minor 20-year or so lapse seems to be a glitch that I'm ironing out quite nicely. And I double dare you to disagree...

## Think fast, slowly
*Alan Smith, 15th June 2023*

Time. The ultimate pressure point. The one thing we never have enough of and maybe the most undervalued variable we have to play with in our lives.

I guess that's why we are tempted to misuse it. To waste it perhaps. Or to leap to conclusions without thinking and make a hash of things that may force us to backtrack or unpick poor decisions. Or lose out through misunderstanding or expediency.

Little experiment for you.

A bat and a ball cost £1.10. The bat costs a pound more than the ball. How much is the ball?

If you are like most people you will have said 10p. That's because the fast-thinking part of your brain leapt into action, the cognitive system you used processed the information without engaging. This 'System 1' is the thing that reacts instinctively and impulsively.

The ball actually cost 5p. Think about it.

How about this? Quick answer please.

How many animals of each kind, that's how many animals of each kind, did Moses load onto the Ark?

If you said two, re-read the question.

If you still don't get it, look it up on Google. Moses had nothing to do with the Ark.

Aside from these being fun little word games, they highlight a fascinating point about how our brains work. Engaging the 'System 2' part of our thinking process requires us to slow down, engage the brain and actually think about what is being said or delivered and then make decisions based on a higher level of understanding.

This is even more tricky when dealing with conflicts or with people who have different objectives and drivers than the ones we have. It is exacerbated when we feel under threat or emotional, maybe even angry at how the people we deal with are making demands of us.

So what do we do?

Well, first listen to understand, don't just wait for the breaks in their language to fill with your own thoughts (most probably created before they said anything). Ask questions. Clarify understanding. Ask them to summarise or repeat what they need or want.

Buy yourself some time to think, take a time out, or take someone with you to an important meeting/discussion who can help buy time for you and help clarify understanding for both sides.

My woodwork teacher said it best back in my school days. Measure twice and then cut once. Great advice. And the best use of limited time.

Wish I'd understood the value of it all those years ago.

# Sliding windows
## Ellis Croft, 23rd November 2023

Earlier this year I had one of my window frames fixed under guarantee. Not particularly exciting, nor ostensibly relevant to a negotiation-themed blog. Although to be fair, the repair took place 22 years after the installation. Oh, and 12 years after the expiry of the ten-year guarantee that was the standard offer...

How did this come to pass? Back in 2001, having decided to make an investment in my home, I looked around for a reputable and reliable company to engage in replacing my home's windows. Using a combination of the new-fangled internet search capability offered by exciting upstarts Google (ridiculously I maintained for far too long that they would never usurp the superb search offering of Alta Vista*, but that's why I am not a tech investor) and recommendations from family and friends, I invited quotes from two companies. Both struck me as being entirely acceptable options given my objectives and budget, and their quotes were broadly comparable. How to choose? During a visit from one, the representative was talking me through the benefits of his company's products when he asserted that their quality was such that while the guarantee offered as standard was ten years – industry standard – they would easily outlast that and be good for 25

*For younger readers, Alta Vista was the pre-eminent search engine of the early to mid-1990s. You used to access it using Netscape**

**For younger readers, Netsc... Oh, you get the picture...

years at the minimum. Once upon a time, I may have wearily taken this assertion as typical sales hyperbole (especially as I was a sales professional myself and familiar with such approaches). However, I had spent the previous handful of years burnishing several skills and techniques I had learned on a particular training course. So, rather than rolling my eyes and thinking, 'Well, you *would* say that', I took a different tack. Instead, I asked whether given this admirably robust lifespan it would therefore be a simple and easy request to agree to extend the guarantee to 25 years, instead of the ten on offer. Seemingly surprised that he'd been listened to and heard, the representative said he'd need to check. 'If you were able to get that agreed, I think I'd almost certainly choose you instead of company X,' I suggested. An extra dollop of motivation to get the sale over the line. It worked.

Fast forward to 2023 and having emailed a scan of the guarantee (amazingly they were sceptical I had the guarantee for 25 years so required evidence – to be fair they acted in entirely good faith subsequently) I benefitted from a repair that would have been painfully costly in the absence of this guarantee. For a negotiator there are perhaps two lessons: firstly, that listening is a skill that you can develop because it will benefit you in a number of ways. Secondly, that value is relative – an extended guarantee wasn't on my agenda as an objective, but as the opportunity arose it was a good idea to take it. I'm glad I did, as its value increased as time passed. The training course that prompted this behaviour? Modesty forbids. But suffice to say that as well as making the organisations I've worked for a substantial sum in savings and incremental revenue, it's done pretty well for me as well.

# Back off!

## David Bannister, 28th March 2024

There's a lot in the media at the moment about 'bullying'. It seems that often when you challenge a point of view there is a risk that the challenge could give rise to an accusation of bullying. When we ask people about which negotiating situation they find most challenging they often tell us it involves aggressive behaviour. The use and abuse of power is a significant issue in life. People who are bigger, stronger, more experienced or further up the organisational hierarchy can use their power positively and negatively. Abusing power to the detriment of others is today often described as 'bullying' even though the original meaning of a bully was a 'sweetheart'.

People abuse power because doing so works for them. When we assess the power balance, we may judge that we are in a less advantageous position (although we often underestimate our own power). If you think that you have the balance of power and that your goals are aligned, then you should explore ways of achieving mutually beneficial outcomes – adopt a collaborative approach. If you feel that although goals are aligned, the other party has the greater leverage, then seek to demonstrate that you can bring to the negotiation things that the other party values – that way, you can contribute and get an outcome that benefits you.

The problems usually arise when the other party wants their own way and sees crushing you as a legitimate means of getting it. Remember, complete powerlessness is very rare – you usually have something the other party wants and aggression is mostly a tactic. People use tactics because they work for them – bullies bully because they have got away with it before either with you or with others.

Abuse of power is usually determined by where your interests lie in relation to the activity. Recently, a council meeting setting a budget was halted by a loud pro-Palestinian demonstration in the council chamber. One of the councillors then tried to push one of the demonstration leaders out of the chamber. I am sure if you asked either of these players which of them was abusing power, they would both say it was the other party and that they were acting entirely within their rights. In a similar way to other negotiating issues, it is never a bad thing to try your best to see the things you plan to do from the other party's perspective.

As with many issues, good communication is key. When you negotiate with an aggressor, be very clear about what you want to achieve; where you might be willing to be flexible and, importantly, where you are not. Very critical to all of this is avoiding emotions – remember the quote from George Bernard Shaw, 'Never wrestle with a pig, you both get dirty and the pig enjoys it!'. Don't be drawn in to the temptation to use similar tactics back because they are almost certainly better at it than you; they have had more practice. Keep things factual, describe the behaviour they exhibit and what effect it has on you and others then prescribe different behaviour for the future always avoiding evaluative expressions – accusing someone of being unreasonable, belligerent or a bully will just make them more so because it focuses on the emotion and not the facts. And the more you do it the more likely the real issue of the negotiation is to get lost in the ensuing scrap. It is also helpful to make a timeline for improvement and to monitor it regularly.

Newspapers may have us believe that workplace bullying is more common than it has been – it probably isn't, but if we encounter it, we need to treat it as we would if we met it in a negotiation – recognise it, call it out by describing it and propose better behaviour. Your assertiveness balances the power with the aggressor and promoting your strength brings positivity back. Aggression, as anyone on a Scotwork course will tell you, very often leads to deals that are not optimal as the outcome is achieved without cooperation or real commitment to the outcome because no one ever made themselves great by showing how small someone else is.

## Negotiating space
*David Bannister, 4th May 2023*

Recently, Elon Musk's interplanetary ambitions were thwarted when his SpaceX starship was launched and very rapidly exploded. I listened to this on my radio with only passing interest (I am of an age that allowed me to watch man land on the moon for the first time and nothing has quite matched it since). But my attention was piqued when a Musk spokesman described the event as a 'rapid unscheduled disassembly'. Somehow that sounds far more technical and less apocalyptic than 'it blew up' but that is no doubt what they meant.

At about the same time, the UK Deputy Prime Minister, Dominic Raab, chose to resign after an inquiry by a barrister, which suggested that some (but by no means all) civil servants claimed to have been bullied by him. I don't know about you but in my lifetime, I have worked for some tough bosses – one of whom is now a knight of the realm and one a member of the House of Lords. These people set very high and very exacting standards for themselves and for those who worked for them. They felt that any failure on my or my colleagues' part was a failure on their part, too. Inevitably there are times when you miss the performance mark and you can be confident that these demanding bosses don't let that event slide by without comment. In my experience of this – which I am pleased to tell you was not too frequent – it was treated as something from which I could learn. I was asked what I thought of my project or piece of work and then subjected to probing questions that resulted in me saying, 'Well, yes, looked at like that it should have been better/clearer/more cogent' and so on. Interestingly, the conversations usually started with the boss saying something like, 'I want to understand your thinking here' or 'Can we discuss the implications of this for the client…'. The suggestion of course was that I had not thought it through or that I had not taken the client's perspective. But I entered into the conversation reasonably willingly, knowing that it would probably challenge me but not belittle me – I would be needed again the next day! I was always chastened but never, ever felt bullied. I learned and did not do it twice!

The reaction to the Raab affair has been varied, but at one extreme there has been an implication that those on the receiving end of the behaviour were weak 'snowflakes' unable to tolerate criticism. I can't comment, I wasn't there, but if the boss's critique was a justified one – that work was not well or properly carried out, as Raab has suggested – can we draw any lessons?

Here is one. When we speak in a situation that is emotionally charged, has high stakes or is threatening, there is a significant risk that we may be misunderstood. This misunderstanding is not about what we say, but about what those we say it to may conclude about *what we mean* by what we say and what is the intention behind our words. If I say to someone, 'Your recommendations were not in accordance with policy and you should know that', the recipient is likely to be immediately *en garde*. Why? Because the implication is that they think I am suggesting that they may have been any one of stupid, negligent or deliberately provocative, or indeed many other things. They become defensive. The best form of defence can be attack and the stand-off begins.

This is an important human reaction for negotiators to understand – when you say something in a negotiation, an event which will often meet the emotionally charged, high stakes criteria, the person you speak to not only hears you but is also likely to ask themselves *why* you said what you did. It is by no means impossible for the answer they give themselves when considering your motive to be that you are disagreeing, challenging, even intimidating or bullying. You had no such intent but because you lazily require them to define your motive for themselves they choose the worst one and, very importantly, the consequence is often that the tone you wished to have in the discussion becomes much less amicable or collaborative.

It takes practice, but it is worth ensuring that in key moments in negotiations, you indicate why you are saying something: 'Perhaps you can help me to understand...', 'Can you clarify...' and 'Will you take me through your thinking on...' are among the many simple behavioural expressions you can use to defuse a potential misinterpretation and its time-consuming and often damaging consequences. And remember, the one time when you invariably indicate your motive is when you say, 'I disagree...', which is always certain to put people on the defensive thus proving that no rule will always apply! Give your factual reasons for disagreeing first.

Try to use these hints to prevent your negotiations from experiencing a rapid unscheduled disassembly or crashing and burning as most of us would probably say.

## The sooner the better...
*Horace McDonald, 24th August 2023*

It has long since been remarked that we're in the golden age of television and I have to admit that I watch a lot of it. I work from the bottom of my garden, so even on a long working day, I have plenty of free time to indulge. I don't need to be out every night; the kids have left home and my wife also works from home. We like watching TV together (have I mentioned I also watch a lot of football?), we rarely if ever binge and typically have three-ish series on the go at any one time and watching these together is sacrosanct. Whilst our kids are no longer at home, between us we share a lot of messages about the things we all like and make recommendations.

We've taught them well. It never ceases to amaze me when I encounter people who don't watch TV, but as they say, there's nowt stranger than folk.

We've recently finished watching the second season of *The White Lotus,* an American black-comedy drama series that follows the guests and employees of the fictional eponymous hotel chain and takes place across a week of new guest arrivals. The first series was set in Hawaii and the second in Sicily. Both seasons tease the end of the series at the very beginning, but there are sufficient twists and turns to disavow the viewer from working out the plot (even for my wife). The original press release for the series states that 'each passing day, a darker complexity emerges in these picture-perfect travellers, the hotel's cheerful employees and the idyllic locale itself'. The show was created, written and directed by Mike White, who created 2003's wonderful *School of Rock* film with his mate Jack Black.

The show's dark underbelly is in stark contrast to the amazing beauty of *The White Lotus* hotels. Whilst each of the guests arrive mostly independently, sometimes as couples, sometimes with friends, their journeys and stories intertwine with the some of the other guests and also with the staff, thus revealing the personal issues they are seeking to escape from – a bit like how we use our 8-step framework to distil negotiation; the seven deadly sins (pride, greed, wrath, lust, envy, gluttony and sloth) are very much the feature here. Having just typed 'the seven deadly sins' into Google, the first thing that appeared on the search result was its link to *White Lotus* and a series of videos connecting the two that has 12m views on TikTok. There was me thinking I was the first person to have made the connection!

Each guest's journey becomes increasingly perilous as their excesses and peccadillos, often linked to their extreme wealth, have greater chance to be exploited. Two examples spring immediately to mind. In the first, Tanya McQuoid (a rich, needy, self-absorbed heiress) the only character who appears in both series brilliantly, is charmed by a wealthy British expat Quentin who whisks Tanya and her assistant Portia off to his sumptuous villa for a party he is holding with a number of (gay) friends. By this point, Portia had previously been seduced by Quentin's nephew Jack. All seems well until Tanya is woken on the first night by noises coming from another room and sees Quentin and Jack engaged in sexual congress, thus suggesting that the relationship and their motivations are not as originally stated. Later Tanya comes across a picture whilst surreptitiously exploring Quentin's bedroom, which suggests a possible connection between her husband (who mysteriously left the holiday early) and Quentin. At breakfast the following morning, Tanya made mention of the fact to Portia that the relationship between Quentin and Jack was questionable but chose not to provide any facts. This lack of disclosure has significant implications for the rest of their journey, which you'll only know if you watch it. Yes, I know it's only a TV programme; however, the show is littered with examples such as this. The second highlights two couples who have travelled together (the husbands were at Yale together) who spent a night apart as one of the wives had booked a similarly opulent hotel as a mini-break within a break and the other wife who'd accompanied her comes back to find potentially incriminating evidence that could question her husband's fidelity (he was innocent) but rather than telling the truth (the character never lied to his wife) he further imperilled their increasingly fractious relationship by being economical with the truth.

At Scotwork, we believe that if you have bad news that you need to give the other party, tell them early. There is little to be gained from withholding it. By revealing it late you damage trust, decrease the opportunity for the other party to be part of the solution and it puts you on the back foot, which is a place you never want to be as a negotiator!

The third season is based in Thailand, we can't wait…

## Biden bows out
*Ellis Croft, 25th July 2024*

The unwinding of Joe Biden's re-election campaign came to its conclusion over the weekend, as the President withdrew his presumptive nomination as Democratic candidate in this November's US election. This process brutally illustrates the win/lose nature of politics (which we saw on this side of the pond on 4th July) and gave me pause for thought. Politics at election time is inherently competitive – the objective is to win power, almost always at the expense of a rival. Negotiation offers us a different possibility, however – that counterparties may have the ability to emerge from a conflict mutually satisfied, rather than as victor or defeated.

Of course, not everybody sees negotiation that way. Donald Trump, for example, sees negotiation very much as being all about 'winning' and there's little doubt that his ultra-competitive approach has seen him take advantage of some remarkable deals (the story about how he exploited a seller's dire financial situation to obtain a $30m 727 airliner for a mere $8m being just one example). However, the drawback with such a competitive approach is the significant risk it brings when dealing with those we want to be negotiating with on a repeated basis over time. For the majority of us who negotiate commercially, most of the time we would probably see a collaborative approach as being more strategically sound and beneficial.

Being collaborative with those we negotiate with is something that we explore in detail on our courses, but there are a number of ways that we can foster an atmosphere of cooperation in our negotiations, should it be in our interests to do so (on which, we also examine competitive behaviours so that negotiators can make their own choice, and execute skilfully, in either scenario). Some of these ideas can be usefully applied in situations where a relationship is currently adversarial but your preference would be to engender a collaborative approach. A tactic I used successfully involved looking at how I treated information in my negotiations. Firstly, I'd compare how I disclosed information in two different relationships: one being a poor, competitive relationship and one where trust was implicit. Frequently I'd find that in the latter I was invariably open and transparent, and this was reciprocated in good faith – exactly what I wanted as it helped us work towards mutually beneficial deals. With the former on the other hand, I'd most often find that my information sharing was scant to non-existent – I feared (rightly or wrongly) that anything I shared, however basic, would somehow be used to undermine my position. To change this dynamic, I would consider what information I could share (that I previously did not) in a competitive relationship that would have no risk and share that. Over a relatively short period of time it would become clear whether the other party was attempting to use this information for competitive advantage, or whether they were reciprocating by sharing non-contentious information they previously would have held back. If my information sharing was reciprocated, then I'd up the ante and start to share information that did expose me to risk, but in a limited way – again, to test the water. If that was used against me, simple enough to dial back down my sharing of information. If, on the other hand, my counterparty started to share information with me that exposed them to risk, then I knew that we were moving towards a relationship where collaboration was not only a possibility, but a probability. It hopefully goes without saying that where the other party did share contentious information with me, I would be sure to not use that in a competitive manner to gain advantage! As a process this may take time, but if your objective is to transform an adversarial relationship into one where you can collaborate, the investment is worthwhile.

In US politics, the binary outcome on offer creates competition meaning a substantial minority will inevitably be disappointed come November, but an outcome that leaves both parties comfortable and – crucially – committed to the implementation of deals is one that is in the interests of many negotiators.

# Hyperbole

## Stephen White, 6th April 2023

Every reader who has experienced adolescents will be familiar with teenage hyperbole. This normally involves taking a premise and stretching it to an unimaginable extreme, in the hope that the resulting conclusion will influence the parent. I discovered the syndrome as a perpetrator. When I was 16 years old, I told my father that I *had* to have a pair of winklepickers (a style of shoe pioneered in the 1950s) because 'everybody wears nothing else'. My father was unmoved. 'Look down and learn,' he said, pointing to his own respectable black brogues.

I took the point. Far from achieving my objective of making a statement that was irresistibly persuasive, I instead rendered my assertion laughably incorrect, and at the same time cast doubt on any future data I might bring into my argumentation.

So it was with Donald Trump yesterday when he told his supporters after his court appearance that every single pundit and legal analyst had said there is no case against him. Not only is this demonstrably untrue but it has no persuasive value, not even to those who accept everything that Donald Trump says as gospel because they just don't care one way or the other. You will no doubt be reminded of his claim that his inauguration in 2017 was attended by the biggest crowd in the history of the event, when it was clearly demonstrable that the crowd at Barack Obama's inauguration was substantially bigger.

My antennae were sensitised to the phenomenon of hyperbole recently when a colleague who was presenting a marketing report commented on some of the claims made by other players in our sector. 'Training by the World's Best Negotiators'. 'Nobody Does it Better'. 'The best negotiation training available anywhere'. And so on. I am intrigued to know what prospective clients think about this sort of exaggeration; I have no doubt studies have been done, which indicate a positive response sometimes happens, but personally I can never get excited by it. It's just silly; partly because there is no reliable database on which to make these assertions, and partly because it indicates lazy thinking – just say any old thing that sounds impressive.

My dad wasn't persuaded by my hyperbole. I don't think there are many people who believe Donald Trump – even his supporters know he is often a stranger to the facts; they just don't care. And here at Scotwork we will continue to strive to make marketing claims that are supported by data and meaningful to our clients.

## Do you feel lucky?
*Alan Smith, 3rd August 2023*

Talking to an old mate over the weekend caused me to once again consider the role that luck plays in many aspects of our lives.

He told me the unbelievable story of one of his colleagues who he claimed was possibly the unluckiest person he had ever known. It was so bizarre that it had to be true. You certainly could not make it up.

He told us that on one journey of less than 50 miles, she had experienced no fewer than eight accidents. That on the way to her wedding she heard fire engines going to the church that was burning down taking with it all of her flowers and orders of service. That her father flooded her house when trying to mend a ballcock in her loft water tank and her mother had set fire to the kitchen when cooking.

I subsequently googled 'unluckiest person in the world' and realised that whilst she was certainly not blessed with good fortune there are a lot who have experienced far worse. Take a look if you don't believe me.

In his book *Quirkology*, Richard Wiseman, an eminent professor in Psychology, talks about an experiment he ran with groups of people, some of whom self-described themselves as lucky and others unlucky.

In the experiment, the two groups were given a newspaper and asked to go through it page by page and count how many colour photos had been used in the articles.

Both groups completed the task and had accurately measured the photos.

If you are ever asked to participate in a psychology experiment by the way never assume the task they give you to superficially respond to is the real purpose. What had also happened is that hidden in plain sight in the paper was an ad that read, 'Tell the psychologist running the experiment you have seen this ad and you will receive £100.'

The group that had claimed they were lucky had a significantly higher rate of seeing this ad and claiming their £100 reward. Seems that luck is in the way that you see the world to a greater degree than how much luck is actually available. Or as Shakespeare would say, 'There is nothing either good or bad, but thinking makes it so.'

The optimistic negotiator in me sees this as one of life's great lessons. Entering into any of life's conflicts with a hopeful and open mind will significantly expose my own eyes to the areas of possibility to create outcomes I can live with – and will also help me recognise when outcomes that are not possible are best left to explore other avenues that may be more fruitful.

The closed and myopic world is a dark and dismal place.

Practice being lucky people.

I'm off to buy a Lottery ticket.

# Question mark
*Horace McDonald, 30th May 2024*

In the last two years my wife and I have treated ourselves to a bit of winter sun. She needs it more than I do and it certainly helps to break up the monotony of the British winter and this year's has been a particularly miserable one.

We were on an island much frequented by the British and I settled down in one of two restaurants in the complex we were staying in to watch Liverpool versus Chelsea compete in the EFL (English Football League) Cup Final. I had a table by myself and in front of me were three men (who I later discovered were Wigan FC fans) and a young man behind me who supported Spurs. Whilst watching the game, it became clear that the adjacent restaurant was also showing the game, which was confirmed when we heard a shout when Liverpool scored and realised that the feed to the other restaurant was slightly ahead of ours. On spotting the young man who was watching the game sporting his (slightly too small) Liverpool shirt, we asked him to come over to us and he duly obliged and sat with me.

The young man Mark (not his real name – I've always wanted to write that) was neurodiverse and we ended up forming quite a bond. His way of communicating was primarily by asking lots of very direct questions, which I found rather refreshing. We shared information about where we lived, whether I'd stayed at the compound previously and he was particularly interested on why I wasn't consuming alcohol at the same rate as the others nearby.

Mark left the table towards the end of the game as he was being picked up by his parents with whom I had a brief conversation. It was pleasing when one of the Wigan fans complimented me on how good I'd been with Mark.

The art of good questioning is fundamental to negotiation. At Scotwork we hold very dear the importance of understanding the other party's position and to do this we need to prepare and ask lots of questions, which not only provides information, but also enables us to test the assumptions we have made in preparation. People often find questioning difficult, either because they fear that they will get an unfavourable response or that they feel they are imposing. Questioning is one of the traits that children are more comfortable with than adults, much like their ability to see the word 'no' as the start of a persuasion exercise rather than the end.

As negotiators we have a choice to make as to whether we are direct or more considered in our questioning approach, and it's important to moderate this depending on how we expect our counterparty to respond to these different approaches. Mark did not appear to have that luxury and understanding and not being offended by it was key.

Mark's shotgun approach to questioning was exemplified when he walked past me by the pool the following morning...

'Did you go out for dinner last night...?'

'What did you eat...?'

'Was it good...?'

'What's your favourite food...?'

'Did you have anything to drink with it...?'

'What did your wife have to eat?'

'Did she have a drink...?'

Etc....

Whilst the person on the receiving end may have felt a little challenged by Mark's barrage questioning technique, it worked for him and as we'd already had a relationship, it was more than fine by me. Always better to ask the question than not, as you never know what you might learn, good or bad, and if it's the latter, the earlier you know the answer the better able you will be to finding a solution...

## Power play

*Ellis Croft, 25th April 2024*

During most of our recent courses many participants have raised the issue of leverage, or power, in their negotiations in relation to the challenges they lean into on a day-to-day basis. It's a topic that's well worth reviewing and on a regular basis – there's plenty to think about.

On the most simplistic level, power can be determined by factors that most of us have little or no control over: size, turnover, resources, dependency, authority and more. On another level, power is nuanced – politicians may be small in number (compared to many of the interests with whom they may negotiate) but their ability to project authority through legislation more than compensates for that.

Sometimes, however, power can be very much within our control. We see this with increasing frequency in the UK as the inevitable election, which must be held by January 2025, draws ever closer. Powerful politicians suddenly realise that their dependency on parliamentary power is contingent on our votes – for a brief period, the electorate collectively has a higher leverage over the fortunes of the nation than is normally the case.

Similarly, there are some fascinating arguments taking place in the USA over unionisation within the automotive sector. The United Auto Workers Union (UAW) have been canvassing the workforce at Volkswagen's (VW) Tennessee plant for a long time to join them – this invite has been rejected by the workforce twice previously. This month, however, the anticipation is that the next vote may well see workers vote in favour of unionising. The arguments for? Job security, higher wages, better conditions and benefits. Counter balancing what would appear to be attractive arguments for those on the shop floor are concerns that unionisation would increase costs, throttle investment and scare off automotive manufacturers who enjoy the benefits of US employment laws as they stand. In what has long been a traditionally Republican voting state, these arguments have held sway. So what's changed? One view being espoused is that the pandemic has changed the dynamic as workers view the precedent set by employers laying off workers during Covid as representing a new and existential threat to their employment. Another is that UAW strike action won workers significant concessions at Ford, General Motors and Stellantis in 2023, credible evidence that collective action can deliver concrete results. As a negotiator, the response to this of VW, Mercedes and Nissan fascinates me; they increased workers' salaries, apparently unconditionally. On the one hand, this action could be seen to rob the UAW of a big chunk of their power – the ability to offer the prospect of a better livelihood. On the other hand, it could be interpreted as a signal from the manufacturers that the workers could have enjoyed better pay all along – had they been unionised. Of course, this may have the unintended consequence of conferring more power to the UAW, rather than less. And most interesting of all is that we won't know until the VW workers vote whether the pay increase added to the power of the company or the UAW, because right now, the power balance actually sits with the workforce. So while power can often be seen as beyond the reach of the individual, this is not always so – and equally importantly, power is dynamic. It moves and grows and diminishes – whether through cycles, external factors or the actions of individuals.

# CHAPTER 3

# READING AND RESPONDING TO SIGNALS

As negotiations develop, even in the most collaborative scenarios, people can become entrenched around intractable decisions or demonstrate inflexibility. Humans are competitive and this can lead to making what we call absolute statements, where they take seemingly fixed positions. You can expect a change in language to qualified statements as the negotiation develops, which can be associated with increased flexibility. This can also be characterised by the other party asking questions about a previously intractable issue, which typically signals flexibility.

As well as tone and approach, their posture and the language they use can help you to understand their true feelings on an issue.

Signals are welcome and they indicate flexibility. It's important to be alert and recognise them. Crucially, build trust *reward* signals – don't punish them.

## Get the picture?
### David Bannister, 14th September 2023

For as long as I can remember, I have enjoyed the work of the Bradford-born artist, David Hockney. Now 86 years old, his work has shown a level of innovation and creativity which I consider to be unmatched. His perception, use of colour and approach to new media have kept his work fresh and captivating over the years. He has used various paint types, photography and now the iPad to produce his unique images. In 1989, he designed the cover of the Bradford telephone directory and these are still in plentiful supply but change hands for upwards of £40 on eBay – for a telephone directory over 30 years old! His most expensive painting to date sold at auction for more than £80m.

I met Hockney very briefly at Los Angeles Airport some years ago when I was able to say to him how much I enjoyed his work. He was gracious in acknowledging my approach. One of my treasured possessions is a book of his work signed for me by the artist. I have been to several of his exhibitions and am planning a return to the permanent exhibition of his work in Salt's Mill near Bradford where his

90-metre-long painting, *A Year in Normandy*, is currently on display.

Much of the artist's work represents the area in which he lived at the time: California and East Yorkshire feature significantly as he has spent time in both. He now lives in Normandy where he has purchased an old farm building and constructed a studio from which he works. He still paints for seven or eight hours a day and his prolific output is testimony to this dedication. Melvyn Bragg recently did a series of interviews with Hockney in Normandy to discuss his work and the extensive iPad paintings he is now doing featuring his local environment. Hockney, even at his age, remains rebellious and challenging – the round spectacles are still a feature along with his loudly checked suits and the crocs he wears on his feet. He still smokes cigarettes and in response to criticism of this and many other things, wears a badge which says, 'End bossiness soon', as to say 'End bossiness now' would be 'too bossy'.

In his interview, he recalls sitting in Normandy painting some trees (he paints lots of trees) and tells of a man who came past him while he was working over several days. Eventually, the man asked him why he spent so much time painting trees. Hockney replied that he loved painting trees as part of the landscape. The man apparently said that he could not understand why, as trees are 'all the same'. Hockney was incredulous and explained that he could sit for days painting trees because he loves to pick out the nuances and uniqueness in each one – colour, shape, species and variations due to the season. This approach and dedication are evident in his latest major work painted in Normandy – you can see it on YouTube and decide for yourself.

What has this to do with negotiating? As I watched the Bragg interviews, I was reminded that one of the skills of a negotiator is to listen and to watch. We should be constantly on the alert for nuances, for differences in tone, in emphasis and in apparent priorities. We should be conscious of gestures and posture that may give clues about the significance which our counterparties attach to aspects of their negotiating position and their responses to what we say. Giving these things our acute attention will allow us to understand better our counterparty and to check, question, follow up and formulate our response. Different negotiators on different days addressing different issues are as distinct as a French oak tree in cold December or sunny July. Our Capability Survey at Scotwork tells us many negotiators are generally not good at listening, paying attention and reflecting back to check their understanding. So, give as much of your attention when you negotiate as David Hockney gives to the trees he paints – it's the differences you spot that provide you with the best opportunities and the fullest picture.

## A negotiator's crystal ball?
*David Bannister, 11th July 2024*

As I write, it is Sunday 7th July. Last week, the UK saw a widely predicted change of government. I am going to look at a negotiation that is yet to happen as a result of the election, consider the important factors in play and try to predict what might result.

A couple of weeks ago, while listening to the news on the car radio, I said to my wife that within a few days of the new government taking office, the new Health Secretary, who I correctly predicted would be Wes Streeting, would have a meeting to attempt to negotiate an end to the long period of industrial action taken by the English junior doctors called by their representatives in the British Medical Association (BMA). To refresh your memory the English junior doctors have been in dispute with the government for almost two years over their pay resulting in strikes and an acrimonious stand-off.

The new Health Secretary wasted no time in pronouncing the NHS to be 'broken' – an interesting choice of words as I always thought that when something was broken it would no longer work. I suspect that this is a tactical choice of expression allowing Streeting to eventually claim he has mended the service (even if that proves to be debatable). Nevertheless, my prediction was correct and the Secretary of State has arranged to meet the junior doctors this week. This gives me the opportunity to speculate about what might happen and to look at the variables and tactics here.

First of all, the fact of the government calling a meeting may be a tactical victory for the doctors because the previous Secretary of State refused to meet them when they were staging strikes. Arranging the meeting is, in itself, then, a signal of intent – Streeting wants a deal perhaps because a negotiated return to normal working by the junior doctors can be heralded as a start to the 'mending' process. I am confident that the junior doctors have an expectation that this new government will be more willing to deal than the last one. However, interesting issues remain. Significant amongst these is the matter of precedent – important in negotiations. Precedent can, of course, be both followed and created. There is precedent here as the Scottish and Welsh junior doctors have settled their pay claims by agreeing a 12.6% increase with the relevant devolved governments. Allowing the Secretary of State to ask, if he dare, 'Explain to me please, why a doctor's work is more valuable in England than it is in Wales or Scotland.' Also, hospital consultants have made a deal of between 12.6% and 19.6% with a restructuring of their pay arrangements meaning that they earn more faster than they did previously and thus introducing the infinitely flexible variable of *time* – more of this in a moment.

What signals do we read here? The junior doctors cited 15 years of not keeping up with inflation and claim that a pay increase of 35% is necessary to restore their relative position. There are a number of things about this. First, you can calculate their 'loss' using different and equally valid measures of inflation and arrive at different outcomes. Second, nobody, not even the most delusional optimists on the Junior Doctors' Committee of the BMA believes that they will end up with close to 35% now with settlements of 12.6% elsewhere – the precedent that would create would be a hole through which nurses, consultants, auxiliary staff and all of the other NHS employees from radiologists to physiotherapists would leap without needing invitation, not to mention the junior doctors in Scotland and Wales and, probably the rest of the UK public sector. However, the English junior doctors' representatives have said that any offer has to be 'credible' but, unhelpfully, have failed to define what that means so that if they arrive at a settlement they will be free to recommend it to their members as being 'credible', risking, perhaps, the possibility that their claims have raised members' expectations to an unachievable level. However, the first thing that Streeting should do at his meeting this week is get them to define 'credible' if he can. If he can't then testing the water with an offer might be the way in which he flushes out that elusive definition. The current, rejected offer is 11.8% made by the previous government leaving precious little room for movement before the 12.6% accepted and implemented elsewhere is exceeded and we get into precedent creating territory. So here, Streeting may be able to use the variable of time. He is quoted as saying, in a very significant negotiating signal, that this will be a 'journey not an event'. In a very important reciprocal signal, the junior doctors' reps have indicated the possible acceptability of 'phasing in' a deal allowing for a possible staged agreement.

Looming over all of this, of course, is the credibility of a newly appointed Secretary of State who has spent much time suggesting that he can fix the problem but not with a 35% offer (although he has never suggested a figure which might be possible) thus bringing into play that emotional negotiating issue of loss of face – it is my opinion that he *must* get a deal but has to tread a very fine line between the success of getting an agreement to end a lengthy dispute and the failure of being accused of simply throwing money at the problem.

This fascinating game will be played in a relatively public forum this week. So I shall stick my neck out: no final deal this week – it would look too much like caving in after such a long and cantankerous stand-off. But there will, I think, be a clear indication of 'significant progress', with lots more conciliatory and cooperative noises. The outcome that will emerge soon after will involve more than one stage in the resolution and a deal not too far removed from the Welsh and Scottish ones with more reserved for the future. Some of Streeting's recent public announcements have been about his intention to do what some people call 'sweat the assets' of the NHS – get more from what is there and this may be the opportunity for him to announce the practical beginnings of such a strategy. So I would expect some element of productivity in its broadest sense to be attached, like a good negotiator, as a condition to the phasing in of additional pay. We shall see!

## The sound of silence
*David Bannister, 12th January 2023*

You would have to live in a remote corner of the world to be unaware of the controversy surrounding the British Royal Family as it has unfolded over the last two years. During that time the Duke of Sussex and his wife have participated in an interview with Oprah Winfrey and a six-part television series about themselves. The Duke, Prince Harry, has written an autobiographical book, with some assistance, and appeared in revelatory television interviews to promote its publication. Other books and articles have been written about the pair either with their approval and collaboration or not. During all of this time, the King, the Queen Consort and other members of the family who have been the main subjects of the stories and complaints from the Sussexes have remained almost entirely silent save for the now Prince of Wales declaring that the family was 'definitely not racist'.

## Silence in negotiation

Prince Harry has complained about that silence in his most recent interview (I read about this; I have not watched it). This moved me to think about silence as a negotiating tactic (no, I am not about to advocate that the King opens a negotiation between London and Montecito (where Harry resides) – that is a very different tactical matter). However, when we negotiate, two of the key questions for us to ask ourselves are 'How much do we disclose to the counterparty?' and 'What do we need to ask to complete, as well as we can, our knowledge and intelligence about them?'. Generally, to be able to define what in Scotwork we call 'The Bargaining Arena', we need to establish by questions and disclosure that area of common interest wherein, if there is to be an agreement, it can be built and finalised. An essential part of negotiating is this information exchange to manage expectations and indicate areas where there may be or will not be flexibility. As the former US Secretary of State, Donald Rumsfeld, said, 'There are known knowns – the things we know we know; there are known unknowns – the things we know we don't know; and there are unknown unknowns – the things we don't know we don't know.' This has always struck me as insightful: untested assumptions and incomplete knowledge can be damaging to negotiators, taking them off along a track leading to no mutually beneficial end which, at best, lengthens the process and, at worst, may even lead to deadlock where an outcome might have been achievable.

What about silence, though? Some years ago, an academic told me that silence can be used to an advantage in negotiating. He told me that in most cases a lack of reaction on the part of a negotiator can cause the counterparty to behave in certain ways and he particularly pointed out that maintaining silence by failing to respond could lead to the original party talking too much to fill the empty space of the silence. That filling of the void may be intended to provide the opportunity for repeating and weakening previous arguments, contradictions and even untruths. The very fact of a lack of reaction to an argument or a negotiating point can cause an assumption to be made about why it is met with silence (such assumptions are usually wrong, the academic contended) and so the void gets filled with more justification diluting what may have been a perfectly strong and defensible position. Contemplating the Sussex communications, I thought that the Prince has, to a degree, proved that point. Recently he accused his stepmother, Camilla, among a host of other allegations, of leaking information to the press about his brother's first meeting with her – this is evidentially untrue and the culprit resigned when the source of the unintentional leak was found. A respected historian and journalist has responded saying, 'If he can get that wrong… then one wonders how much else in the book is imagined rather than real.' One error, which seems to be deliberate to reinforce a view about one person, subjects the whole 'mission' to possible compromise. It can be like this when we negotiate.

The academic was making important tactical points about negotiating here: some people will allow you to respond to their silence by filling the void and weakening the arguments you have used and then attack the weak points which you add on. The risk then is that if your weak arguments fall, will your stronger ones follow them in the 'We can't believe a word they say...' tradition? Which may be exactly what the counterparty wants to happen – to make it all go away.

### Royal lessons

Thanks, then, to our royal case study for teaching us these lessons – be sure that you identify the important and influential things of which your counterparty needs to be aware of and which support your position. Make sure that you make these points forcefully and assertively. Never give the opportunity to allow an attack on a weakened argument by misconstruing silence to mean disagreement and diluting your position. Say what you planned to say and then ask what they think. I will leave you to decide if the repetitions and embellishments coming from California strengthen the position of the Sussexes in the minds of those whom they are trying to convince – polls suggest not. Maybe the lesson is that we should never, ever be afraid of the sound of silence – it can be the most effective response sometimes.

## Signal failure?

*Ellis Croft, 23rd February 2023*

The bewildering array of strike action that's been gathering momentum across sectors over the last year or more has – until now – been characterised by a morbid sense of deadlock. The flexibility that allows us to make deals – and without which we cannot – has been lacking on both sides of the table, and if anything, the language used by all parties has tended towards a hardening of position. Most of us would see this as making the resolution of the conflicts less likely, and rightly so.

Very recently, however, a BBC journalist (Chris Mason) was told by one of his senior government sources that 'We won't be putting limitations on these [i.e. upcoming] talks'. In other words, nothing is off the table. This statement – if it is in fact representative of the government position – is a shift, both in tone and in fact. It's what we call a signal – a move, however subtle or indirect, from the absolute to the qualified. And skilled negotiators know that signals are absolute gold, nuggets of flexibility to be sought out and prized. This is particularly the case when the negotiation is a long and hard road.

What to do if you recognise a signal in your own negotiations? First of all, be alert to the reality that it's only a clue that may – or may not – indicate flexibility. Probe, question and confirm. If it does mean that the other party has decided to modify its previous position, that's good news for you – so it's crucial that you reward this flexibility and build upon it. This may be with a potential signal of flexibility on your part, or something else appropriate to the movement being implied.

The Royal College of Nursing has responded to the government's signal with one of their own – deciding to suspend the next planned strike action. It's a good example of rewarding a signal as there's no commitment on their part to stop their action in future, but it does send a positive message back to the government (and of course, other unions). It will be fascinating to see how those other unions respond themselves. The corollary to our advice that signals of flexibility should be rewarded is, of course, that it's a high-risk approach to punish them. In this case that might be to point out the inconsistency in the position, the time it's taken to move, and so on. The probability is that the only outcome achieved here is to make the flexibility on offer vanish and see it replaced with further intransigence. Whether any unions take this approach remains to be seen – I had a train of thought as to which union may punish this particular signal, but I thought I'd shunt it into the sidings. I'm not so good at predictions.

However you feel about the current series of strike actions, observing what's happening as dispassionately as you can, will offer you some valuable insights into your own negotiations, and how you can improve your own outcomes, no matter how different the context may be.

## Not even in the room
*Stephen White, 13th July 2023*

Summer holidays. The kids want to go to the seaside. Mum also wants to be able to fall out of bed onto a golf course. Dad hates the heat and wants to indulge his fascination with all things historical. And he is hoping for change out of £2,000. A family meeting is called. Each faction promotes their preference but there is no meeting of minds, no surrender by any of the parties and scant opportunity for compromise. The meeting breaks down with no agreement. Eventually, mum takes unilateral action and books an Airbnb in Sicily, a 15-minute walk to the nearest beach, a 20-minute drive to the golf course, two hours from historic Palermo, all-in for £3,500, just £1,500 more than the budget, which as the senior breadwinner she offers to cover.

And then they remember grandpa, who always comes with them and wasn't even invited to the meeting. When they tell him of the Sicily decision, he has a hissy fit. He wants to go to Bournemouth!

A similar gathering took place on Tuesday in Vilnius between the representatives of the 31 member countries of NATO. Plus Ukraine's President Zelensky, who wasn't even in the room. When representatives of many countries come together to agree a common position on an issue, there is high potential for a less-than-perfect outcome. Unsurprisingly, the Summit did not go as smoothly as was hoped.

The hot topic of contention is Ukraine's entry into NATO. Every NATO member recognises that this is inevitable; there is no point in the massive support that NATO countries (and others) are giving to Ukraine to help them win against Russian aggression if cementing Ukraine into the Western alliance doesn't eventually happen. The question is when? And what guarantees can Ukraine be given now that it will happen in the future?

The problem is that a guarantee of entry in the future is tantamount to a NATO declaration of war because Russia would view such a guarantee as a de jure award of membership. The conflagration would immediately spread, and neither side really want that. On the other hand, pussyfooting around the issue identifies weakness and prevents the show of strength that NATO want to portray.

Negotiators have several options in this type of scenario. One is unilateral action – like mum booking the Airbnb. It relies on the other parties acquiescing. This is what the USA decided to do on a related matter – the supply of cluster bombs to Ukraine. Another option is deferral; pushing communiques back to the next Summit, or creating a Working Party to examine the pros and cons. Yet another is détente – using a form of words which can be interpreted differently by the different parties. The official statement issued on Tuesday read: 'We will be in a position to extend an invitation to Ukraine to join the alliance when allies agree and conditions are met.' In other words, it will happen – definitely, maybe.

Détente is fine as long as everyone buys into the ambiguity. On this occasion, President Zelensky was initially not satisfied. The (private) bilateral meetings that took place on Wednesday seemed to calm the troubled waters, notwithstanding the UK's Defence Minister Ben Wallace's comments about the expectation of some gratitude from Ukraine for the arms already supplied. President Zelensky must reckon it is better to keep his criticism of the NATO position muted and keep receiving increasing quantities of weapons from the west, albeit not as quickly as he would like (has anyone told him about Amazon Prime?).

So grandpa might not get to Bournemouth this year, but he has discovered online that there is an English pub serving craft beer and pie and mash a short walk from the Airbnb. An uneasy peace reigns.

# 'These are not the droids you are looking for'
*Ellis Croft, 6th October 2022*

There's a scene in the first *Star Wars* film (*Episode IV*, of course) in which our heroes are attempting to smuggle a pair of robots past the evil Imperial troops in their escape from space port, Mos Eisley. As luck would have it, one of our heroes is a Jedi master – and hence capable of some pretty impressive tricks, including mind control. The Imperial troops succumb easily, our heroes pass the checkpoint and make good their escape. Easy as it is to dismiss this sci-fi fantasy as daft fiction, many of us are quite happy to imagine that we too wield the ability to control others' thoughts. Here are three examples that some of our negotiation course participants have attempted.

1. **The MK-Ultra:** A technique named in honour of the CIA's experiments over the decades around the ability to project thoughts over hundreds of miles (through a theoretical process known as 'remote viewing'). Our intrepid negotiator has certainty on their side: 'Well, *I* know what I want – why on earth don't you?'. The other side of the table is never that far away, after all. As the long wait for their thoughts to transmit across the table continued, it does – sometimes – eventually occur that *saying* what they want may well be a better alternative. As indeed it is.

2. **The 'make me an offer':** Sometimes, unsure about where to pitch, or perhaps anxious that their estimate on what was realistic was going to be wildly inaccurate, negotiators

try this technique. Surely it's simple to manoeuvre the other party into a position that would suit them very well indeed – the only problem being that the resulting offer almost always involves a position that suits the other party very well indeed. Usually a significant distance from their own desired position. However, the solution to this problem? *The very British smile.*

3. **The very British smile**: So, the other party have made a proposal so outlandish – and let's be frank, absurd – that our negotiator's only option is to smile politely, thank them and say that there's plenty to think about, right there. Automatically, they'll understand the precariousness of their situation and that the proposal is dead in the water. When, after a period of time, they get annoyed that their proposal remains unaccepted – indeed, there was interest expressed in it – it will be their fault. Realising this, and with sincere apologies, they will make a radically amended proposal (unfortunately, the technique tends to break down at this point, necessitating an alternative means of driving the deal forward, but still). It's a small but interesting insight, but I have observed that being British is entirely unnecessary when it comes to applying this particular technique.

OK, so we're unlikely to *really* think that we're pulling the strings for the other side of the table, but the number of times we observe apparent mind control attempts on our courses? Too many to count. Influencing the other party through nonverbal communication can be an effective part of the mix, so we're not about to dismiss it entirely – but we are all about making sure that negotiators recognise the situations they find themselves in. That they have a range of options from which they can choose to pursue their interests as effectively as they can. Recognising that Jedi mind tricks belong in a different universe can be a good place to start, sometimes.

## The imbalance of power
*Ellis Croft, 6th July 2023*

One of the prerequisites for a negotiation to take place in the first place is that there must be motivation on both sides of the table. In the absence of an answer to the question 'What's in it for me [WIIFM]?' there can be no trading. Persuasion may win the day, or there may be a (long) conversation, perhaps a problem-solving solution might arise, or of course – if one party has enough power – a solution may be imposed.

The various answers to the WIIFM question – be they good things that might happen if we trade, or bad things we'd rather avoid happening should we not – tell us what the balance of power between parties looks like. It's a truism, but most negotiators tend to overestimate the power of the party they're negotiating with at the same time as not fully weighing up their own. This is a habit to be recognised and avoided as it dramatically narrows our understanding of what a good deal may look like.

On a macro scale, we can see how this works through the machinations the EU has been having as member states debate how to accommodate refugees. After years of failing to get member states to agree to quotas, the European

Commission persisted with the idea that a problem-solving approach might pay off and reframed their proposal to allow member states to pay mandatory 'financial contributions' of €20,000 for each refugee not taken in. However, the inheritors of the UK's mantle of awkward squad, Poland and Hungary, said they'd refuse to pay these fines, err I mean contributions. Various media reports signal that the European Commission is looking at the EU funding that both states receive (a combined €17bn) along with measures that would withhold portions of that funding if the recalcitrant member states continue to refuse to come to the table. My view would be that the introduction of this sanction is likely to enable both Poland and Hungary to find some flexibility in their approach that they previously hadn't noticed, but we shall see. If it does work, it's an example of the effective use of sanctions to reinforce the balance of power – from a negotiator's perspective, at least.

Of course, in our own negotiations, we're unlikely to be sitting on top of multi-billion budgets we can use to drive motivation in those with whom we negotiate – but the principle is the same, in this case raising the sanction of something happening that the other party would wish to avoid. Recently, an online order I made with a major supermarket failed to arrive – not particularly dramatic but irritating as I'd managed to place the order within some time-limited offers that added up to a substantial saving. Being the complainant, I proposed that they re-arrange delivery, honouring the order value as it was at the time it was placed. Their response was to say that they were sorry and that they would refund the non-fulfilled order – leaving me with the problem that re-purchasing the same order outside of the offer period would cost a great deal more. I replied by saying that if that was their position, I would cease online shopping with them until I'd spent a minimum of ten times the order value with their competitors before deciding whether to come back, or if they did have some flexibility in fulfilling the order as made, I would be happy to hear back. The delivery arrived six hours later.

Power is not always about the size or financial muscle – it can be relative and being able to see the opportunities that may present can unlock the chance to do a deal that we may otherwise allow to pass us by. Don't do yourself down – you have power!

## Flash Keegan

*Stephen White, 7th September 2023*

I was a nerd as a teenager. You don't need to know all the details but one indicator was that my crowning desire was to possess my own copy of *Encyclopaedia Britannica* (*EB*). Priced (in the 1970s) at a staggering £1,200 for all 25 volumes, it was so far beyond my means that I recognised it was a pipe dream that I would never likely achieve.

One day I responded to an advertisement in *Reader's Digest* (another nerd indicator) for a free book of sample *EB* articles if in return an *EB* salesperson could make an evening sales call at my home. One evening he arrived. I helped him carry the complete set of *EB* from the boot of his car into the house. We put them on the dining room table and he invited me to browse. I entered a transcendental state, fondling the pages, reading snippets of entries on obscure topics, revelling in the quality of the binding and the paper.

In due course, we talked about the different hire purchase and instalment plans. I was newly married, earning buttons, and nothing he could offer was remotely achievable. He was a good salesperson; empathic, determined but not aggressive. Eventually, he realised I was a lost cause, and he eased off the gas. I made him a cup of tea and we talked about his job. I asked if most of his home-visit sales calls turned out the same way as this one. He told me he made on average seven calls a week and successfully converted four of them into sales. He got no salary but the commission rate he earned was good and four sales a week gave him a prosperous lifestyle.

Hang on – two hours earlier I had helped him bring the books in from his beat-up ten-plus-year-old Vauxhall Victor. This was not a car that reflected the lifestyle he claimed. Had he exaggerated his success? Were cars not a status symbol as far as he was concerned? Was he, in reality, struggling to make ends meet?

So I asked him. He said that he had worked out that arriving at a sales visit in a flash car was likely to be counterproductive. For every potential buyer who might be impressed he calculated that there would be many others put off. Ultimately, who was paying for the flash? The customers were shelling out £1,200 for 25 books. I wanted to ask him if he had a Lamborghini parked in his driveway but I didn't. I will never know.

This incident came into my mind as I read about the trials and tribulations of Mrs Gillian Keegan, currently (at least at the time of writing!) Education Secretary. Not because of her wayward attempt at communicating reassurance about defective concrete in school buildings through a pre-recorded video, or her sweary outburst after an interview, but because she continues to flaunt her expensive jewellery, handbags and second homes enabling the press to have a field day and voters to be unsuitably distracted. She needs to meet my encyclopaedia salesperson and learn a lesson about the common touch.

Some negotiators need to learn the same lesson. I once sat in the magnificent office of an advertising agency's CEO in the West End. He said he personally didn't need any negotiation skills training (sic) but he wanted to run a Scotwork programme for his C-suite colleagues and, he said with a certain amount of entitlement, he needed a big discount on our fee. I asked him if he had decided which location the programme would run at. He named the most expensive hotel in the UK; nothing, he boasted, was too good for his management team. That was the end of any discount he might have gotten from me.

CHAPTER 4

# CREATING MOMENTUM THROUGH PROPOSALS

Making a proposal is the best way to move the negotiation forward. In the **Argue** step, people often continue to try to force the other party to see the world the way they see it, which then moves to persuasion that often leads to points scoring, circular arguments and results in the negotiation getting stuck in its tracks.

One way to avoid this malaise is to either make or invite a proposal (with a strong preference for the former). Think of a negotiation as climbing a mountain. There are times for pausing and reflection – where am I, where is the other party and what do I need to do next – and there are times to create momentum and making a proposal is the best way to achieve this. It is our strong belief that any proposal you make should be realistic, where it addresses all the issues discussed, is credible in that it's supported by the facts and is at the other party's limit according to your understanding (or if unknown, the high point of your intend position). You will see from the stories in this book numerous examples of the importance of making a proposal as it sets the agenda and shifts the focus of the negotiation to your perspective; simply put, a proposal beats an argument.

When receiving a proposal, always probe the basis of it. There are a number of ways to respond, including adjournment, making an instant counterproposal, and best of all, by making a considered counterproposal where you build on the other party's proposal.

There are two fundamental styles of negotiation: **competitive** (adversarial) and **cooperative** (collaborative). The factors that influence **competitive** are one-off transactions, where the relationship has been mandated, there are low levels of trust, emotions often run high and the outcomes are *win-lose*, which often results in value erosion. **Cooperative** negotiations are typified by long-term voluntary relationships, trust, tolerance and understanding of the other party's position and is where skilled negotiators like to play and drive *win-win* (value creation) outcomes.

# My kind of proposal this Valentine's

*Siobhan Bermingham, 8th February 2024*

Whether it's dream proposals, hidden needs, wishes unfulfilled, the need for a greater understanding of what your partner is saying, generous offerings, power dynamics or learning how to give them what they want, Valentine's has never reminded me so much of negotiation before.

With the air of love and excitement that Valentine's brings… the negotiation consultant within me can't help but think about my kind of proposals – not the engagement, bent down on one knee with a ring-type. Instead, I refer to clearly defined, detailed proposals where trading and the powerful use of questions have led to a well-structured proposal that meets my needs as well as the needs of the other party.

The big question – not 'will you marry me?' – instead as a negotiator is the focus on understanding what powerful questions you need to ask when negotiating. For example, when faced with pushback on a proposal: 'Under what circumstances would this proposal be acceptable to you?' or 'Which elements of my proposal do you like?'.

Give them what they want this Valentine's, but on your terms. Much like the world of online dating where confusions are reduced when people clearly state what they actually want – if only every dating and negotiation scenario were so honest and upfront. Do you really know what your business partner wants?

Often when a proposal comes on the table, this is merely the way they believe they will get their needs met. But when you really understand what it is that they need, you can often structure a new proposal that not only gives them what they need, but also meets *your needs* – in the kind of mutually beneficial relationship that we all enjoy.

After all, when it comes to negotiating, it's often not just about the deal you make in any one given meeting, but it's about the tone/expectations set for when that business partner comes back to do business with you again and again. Unless of course, you plan for it to be a very short relationship indeed.

Just as with dating, short-term relationships and long-term relationships are approached very differently in negotiations. Shorter-term relationships, when negotiating, can allow for a more competitive approach. Whereas longer-term relationships can often be far more fruitful if a tone of collaboration and trust is created.

Power dynamics is a topic not only reserved for dating, but also for negotiations. Too often we underestimate the power that we have or believe that the other party is in a greater position of power. When you take the time to have constructive dialogue, ask skilful questions and really understand the needs of the other party, you'll soon discover what incentivises them and what sanctions may be at play. When you understand the incentives and sanctions at play, you're much better positioned to negotiate, leveraging the power available.

Valentine's – a time of hope, possibility and affection – along with increased retail prices for any heart-shaped chocolates or even the simplest of flower arrangements. And the increased surge of restaurant demands and the opening of new profit-making opportunities.

What is your style as a negotiator? Do you find yourself delaying the proposal until later, nervous of how it will land or whether it will be rejected? Do you find yourself sweet-talking the business partner in an attempt to draw out a more collaborative tone? Have you succumbed to goodwill gestures to try to move things forward to only find that suddenly those goodwill gestures become expected in future negotiations?

Some smell the scent of love and perfume. As a negotiator, I smell money and an opportunity not to be missed. Whether you're in sales, procurement or you're a customer purchasing products, dining experiences in restaurants, hotels, spa days – always remember to explore the possibility of negotiating a better deal.

## A Messi way to negotiate
*David Bannister, 13th October 2022*

Lionel Messi is arguably one of the best footballers of recent years and perhaps of all time. His record includes virtually all the superlatives of the game – record goal scorer, record trophy winner and seven times winner of the Ballon d'Or (football's equivalent of the best actor Oscar). In 2003, he joined Barcelona and played in the first team almost continuously from 2005 until 2020 when his immensely lucrative contract came up for renewal. Barcelona had a glittering dominance of Spanish and European club football during many of those years and Messi was an essential member of a wonderful team.

Necessarily, of course, the contract renewal required negotiation. Messi's nine key demands for the renewal of his contract have recently been highlighted in the press. They make fascinating reading. Before I give you the details, let me say that, from a negotiating viewpoint, his approach ticks a number of good practice boxes: he thought through what he wanted, he clearly quantified it and he presented his requirements in a proposal. Moreover, I think it is fair to say that the components of the proposal can be categorised as 'creative'. Let's see if you agree. They were:

- A guaranteed three-year extension to add to a new three-year contract – so that when his new contract expired in 2023, it would automatically be extended to 2026.
- A private box at the stadium in Barcelona for his family and the family of another player.
- A 'one-off' €10m renewal bonus – just for agreeing to sign the contract which, if it had similar terms to the contract just ending, would be likely to pay him about €71m a year plus playing bonuses.
- Commission for his brother who is his representative.
- A €10,000 release clause which would be payable by another club if he was to transfer to them during the contract; his release clause under the expiring contract was €700m so it would be easier for him to leave Barcelona under the proposed new terms if another club were to offer him a better deal.
- Reimbursement of all the wages he had agreed with the club to give up during the pandemic (all of the Barcelona players had agreed to this reduction) with interest on the amount foregone.
- A guarantee that if Spanish taxes increased during the contract, he would not lose any net pay.
- A private jet to take him home to Argentina at Christmas.
- A job guarantee for his personal assistant.

I did say it was creative! But those of you who follow the Beautiful Game will know that Lionel Messi has played for Paris St Germain for the last couple of seasons, his contract at Barcelona having not been renewed. If his approach did tick some boxes where did his approach probably fall short? Barcelona have never made public the demands that they were prepared to meet and those that they were not, but as negotiators, we might be willing to offer the little footballing wizard some advice.

First, make realistic proposals. It's just possible that people who see you earning more than one million Euros a week may conclude that you could probably afford to hire your own private jet. Moreover, there is more than a whiff of undesirable precedent for the club here and elsewhere in his proposal.

Second, prioritise your objectives – which of these nine are potential deal breakers and would lead to you walking away? If all nine are deal breakers, don't expect a deal. Understand that negotiation will always require movement from your ideal position so make sure that you are willing to make concessions especially if they lead to you being able to 'win' on the critical issues. Advice for Barcelona would be that if Messi did not prioritise, then they should ask him to do so and then bargain to reduce the list of demands.

Third, learn to trade – Spanish taxes are beyond the club's control so that this potentially open-ended concession might be acceptable if it were changed to become a review of salary before the guaranteed contract extension, if that is important enough to be agreed upon first.

Fourth, the balance of power – judge your leverage correctly and in this case, perhaps he did. Although the relationship with Barcelona ended, Messi did not lack offers from other top teams. So perhaps, when he first wrote the nine-item demand list, it would have been nice to have known that he could continue as a highly paid player in Europe for some time and probably beyond that in the USA Major League Soccer at the end of his career. Having a good alternative to an agreement strengthens your hand and pressures the counterparty.

It must be nice to give what I think I must politely call a 'digital gesture of dismissal', if your boss won't let you take a private jet home and charge it to expenses. I wish!

## Brownie points
*Alan Smith, 29th June 2023*

As any parent will know, whilst we are always proud of our kids, they are rarely anything other than blasé about us.

I can always remember reading David Cameron's (Britain's ex-Prime Minister and disastrous engineer of the Brexit referendum, other views may possibly be held) accounts of going home to his young family after attending a G7 Summit with the most important political leaders in the world. Apparently, he was told by his kids that he was rubbish at reading bedtime stories. Keeping it real! Hard to think too much of yourself with young kids.

My own school of hard knocks was when (if I've told you this before, please humour me) my daughter came home from school and asked me to help with her homework. She was doing A-level biology at the time and I was clearly not helping at all. She said why are my parents so stupid, why can't I live with parents like Rupert (name changed to protect the innocent) whose parents worked on the Human Genome Project.

So, it is with great pleasure and little humility that I offer a story here that for once got a small amount of praise from my youngest daughter for yours truly, the author.

Having just qualified as a doctor she has landed a job at the Queen Elizabeth Hospital in Birmingham. A new(ish) teaching hospital in the UK's second-largest city.

She has been travelling from our home in Sussex looking to rent a flat in the city close to the hospital, and demand, as you may expect, is pretty high.

Having found a flat and in urgent need of securing it, she called me for some advice.

Without being overly dramatic the only time my daughter calls me is when the car has broken down or there are unruly teenagers making a racket nearby (I once arrived at one of my kid's flats in nothing but my boxers to disturb some shifty individuals, which has gone down in legend at the Smiths' house. I assumed they ran away because of my impressive physique but my kids say it was because they thought I was clearly and visibly insane).

The advice she wanted was how to get a better deal on the flat. She said as a so-called negotiation expert, what advice could I offer on how could she negotiate a better rate?

A couple of questions later I realised the price of the flat was not the problem, it was the cost of parking. Both she and her boyfriend had to buy a parking permit for the property and it was quite a bit on top.

My first question was had they asked for a better rate for two cars?

She said no, but was that all I could offer in terms of advice?

I said ask for a discount of 20% on two cars and call me back. Moments later the phone rang. She said they had said no to 20% but offered 12.5%. I said call them back and say that if they could hit the 20% you would pay quarterly in advance.

An hour later she called me to say they had agreed. £50 a month off was nothing compared to the priceless feeling of my daughter saying thanks dad.

What's my point, aside from a little brag?

Well, the two mistakes my daughter made are classic 101 problems. The first is don't negotiate with yourself. Being afraid to ask for what you want or assuming the other side will say no will prevent more deals from being requested than any other in my humble opinion.

The second is what to do when you do not achieve your objective. Think about using concessions to drive a better deal. Paying in advance is not a problem for her as, sadly for me, the 'Bank of Mum and Dad' is still open. But if it drives a need or value from the other side it can really help build a deal that works for both.

By the way, empty nest syndrome is not a problem, it is a blessed release.

## Go extreme or go home
*Tom Feinson, 14th March 2024*

Football financial fair play – whilst being alliteratively fun – strikes me as something of an oxymoron, but there you go. In an effort to curb some of the more outlandish behaviour of

Premier League clubs, Profit and Sustainability Rules (PSR) were introduced in the 2015/16 season. These rules specify that English Premier League clubs are allowed to lose £105m over a three-year spell. Unfortunately for them, Everton recorded losses of £125m. In March 2023, they were referred to an independent commission, who in November imposed upon them a ten-point penalty which, despite a strong start to the season, dropped them into the relegation zone. At the time, almost to a man or woman, the football literati said that this was extreme, that Everton would appeal and the deduction would be reduced to six points. Everton duly appealed. And guess what? The appeal panel has reduced their penalty from ten to six points. They concluded that the independent commission had made legal errors in two areas:

1. Everton had been punished for 'being less than frank' (check out the signal in that phrase) about their new stadium debt; the appeal panel found that whilst the errors were material, Everton had made an innocent mistake.
2. They also said that a six-point deduction was not out of kilter with other available benchmarks.

So, what is the fallout from this? I think it's safe to assume that every club that falls foul of PSR will appeal, given the precedent has been set that if you do you get a 40% reduction in your points deduction. It also appears that the tactic of 'act dumb, be smart' will be increasingly used: 'Oh, I'm sorry, I didn't realise… silly me.' Everton seem to have got away with claiming that they didn't realise that the cost of building their new stadium couldn't be deducted from their allowable losses. Remember, it was the Premier League clubs of which Everton are one, who determined what the rules were in the first instance. As I write, I'm imagining some of the brightest legal minds in the UK developing defences for their multi-billion pound football masters along the lines of 'I'm really sorry we didn't do it on purpose, we are just a bit thick.'

So, what was the point of imposing a ten-point deduction if within three months it's going to be reduced to six, which is what everyone thought it should be in the first place? From a negotiator's perspective, why do people make extreme opening proposals?

Predominantly, it is to influence the limit position of the other party and/or to set up a haggle. On this occasion, I think they were sending a message to a constituent, the government, who in September had reaffirmed their intent to establish an independent regulator for men's elite football. The message being, 'We've got it under control, we can and will take firm action, we can keep our house in order – we don't need government interference.' Time will tell as to how effective they have been. If Nottingham Forest and Everton have points deducted in their upcoming cases, it's likely they will fall into the relegation zone and will no doubt appeal. Based on the current procedure, the outcome of the appeal will not be announced until after the end of the season, which means we won't know who is relegated with certainty when the season finishes. This could politely be described as chaos – and certainly not a good look if you're trying to demonstrate you are in control.

Oh, and hot off the press, Premier League clubs also re-confirmed their commitment to securing a sustainably funded financial agreement with the EFL (English Football League: Championship, League One and League Two; the three below the Premier League in the pyramid system) subject to the new financial system being formally approved by clubs.

This statement came after a meeting of Premier League clubs who had committed to action in relation to funding agreements with EFL. The Premier League are not happy because the EFL finally have some leverage (the threat of an independent regulator) so they are trying to kick this can down the road (technically known as staying in the argue phase) and playing a game of chicken with the EFL and government, who today re-affirmed their commitment to an independent regulator.

In a further bid to show that they are completely in control, they now plan to get rid of PSR in favour a new system allowing clubs to spend 85% of their turnover on wages, etc… what could go wrong?

# Rubbish on the streets of Edinburgh
*Andy Archibald, 4th July 2024*

For those who are getting excited to visit the Edinburgh Fringe Festival in August this year, get ready for a world-leading celebration of theatre, comedy, dance, physical theatre, circus, cabaret, children's shows, musicals, opera, music, spoken word, exhibitions, and events.

And piles and piles of uncollected rubbish lining the streets.

That's because the now seemingly bi-annual deadlock between the bin collectors and the local government body responsible for pay negotiations, Cosla, has begun this week. Bin collectors, represented in the negotiations by trade unions, have rejected a pay increase proposal from Cosla and confirmed their intention to go on strike at the time the world's largest performance arts festival takes place in the Scottish capital.

Two years ago, a bin strike was held for 12 days during the festival, leading to a huge backlog of waste littering the streets of Edinburgh. Following sustained media coverage and widespread embarrassment over the situation, Nicola Sturgeon, the then First Minister of Scotland, stepped in and gave in to all demands tabled by the bin collectors to make the problem go away. An example of the Edinburgh streets at that time:

Except the problem didn't go away. Because now the trade unions negotiating for the bin collectors know all too well that if they push the right buttons – strike during the festival – Cosla or the government will probably give in again and they'll get everything they want. And the same will keep happening.

The challenge for Cosla is they don't have the power to stop the strike if they don't reach an agreement. But that doesn't mean they are completely powerless in the situation. Cosla know the bin collectors want better pay and this is a concession they can make. The key question is do they give it away for free and encourage the unions to keep coming back for more; or make it conditional and get some value in return?

There is a proposal on the table to increase pay 4.2%, staggered over time and valid for 18 months. The response from the unions has been that 'it's not a strong offer'. (For everyone who has done a Scotwork training course, they'll know that this is not a no; it's a signal.)

From the trade union's point of view, if the proposal received isn't acceptable, state specifically what would be agreeable, ensuring it's realistic and stop asking the other side to guess. Being specific and realistic about what you want is always going to be more effective than being vague and asking the other side to make a proposal.

From Cosla's point of view, ask some good questions to understand what's not strong about the proposal. Is it the way their proposal has been presented (i.e. split over 18 months) or is it not enough (if 4.2% is not enough, what is?). And, provided it's realistic, make a further proposal that addresses the objections, gives the bin collectors what they want (again, provided it's realistic) and, most importantly, is clear on the conditions that Cosla will get in return.

This last bit is hard. Most negotiators are usually pretty good at giving away concessions but not so good at applying conditions to get value in return. In this situation, calling off the strike would be a good place to start for Cosla. Agreeing to a period where there will be no requests for better pay or negotiating any future changes now to avoid this annual/bi-annual merry-go-round might be of value to them. Agreeing realistic performance measures and consequences for non-compliance might also be of value, amongst many other things.

Ideally, we'll see progress to break the deadlock over the coming days that doesn't involve Cosla and the government giving in again. That way, all parties can be satisfied, including everyone visiting the festival enjoying a rubbish-free time.

## Two important tactical negotiating lessons

*David Bannister, 20th April 2023*

In recent days, we have heard the results of two union ballots in the NHS. One rejected a pay offer and the other accepted the same pay offer. The offer promised nurses and other NHS staff represented by UNISON – the union which accepted – and the RCN (Royal College of Nursing), which rejected the deal, a pay increase of 5% and a lump sum the size of which depends on grade. Seventy-four per cent of UNISON members voted to accept the deal, whereas only 46% of RCN members indicated their acceptance. I found myself wondering why. The reason may lie in two important tactical aspects of making a proposal. Let me explain.

The original claim was for 19% which, it was said, was 5% above the level of inflation at the time. At a time when pay increases generally were at around 5%, this may seem to be out of line. I will return to this.

The Chief Executive of the RCN, Pat Cullen, had a high media profile from the beginning of the campaign, appearing on television on BBC *Question Time*, where she accused a journalist – who had sympathy with the nurses' cause – of being 'macho' along with the Health Secretary, Steve Barclay. All the members of the RCN received a communication from their union telling them that the claim was 'affordable, sustainable and deserved'. The government refused to discuss the 19% claim and Ms Cullen modified it in media interviews saying that if the government would come to the table she would want to discuss a 10% claim – 9% of the original gone before any formal discussion.

Eventually, after a period of negotiation, both the RCN and UNISON recommended the 5% plus lump sum deal. UNISON communicated with its members and said that the offer 'would boost pay significantly this year and mean a wage increase next year'. The RCN said that 'there comes a point where the other side won't offer any more'. I detected a different tone in those communications.

Ms Cullen has now had to go back and ask for more but has not specified how much more she needs from a government which will not, according to her own letter to her members, offer any more. It remains to be seen whether the withdrawal of emergency, intensive and cancer care has any effect on the government and if it increases public sympathy or not and whether the RCN membership will again support strike action in a second ballot which they are obliged to hold by law.

There are two important negotiating points to be drawn from this sad state of affairs.

The first is the test of the realism of a claim. The fact that the claim had to be almost halved to get both sides to the table indicates, to my mind, that it was never a credible claim. Maybe it was an attempt to be 'macho' to use the RCN's own expression, but anyone with any experience in negotiation could have told them that the tactical issue with wildly unrealistic proposals is that you have to move back from them a long way to get into a space where bargaining can even begin to take place. The result is often a loss of face, which may account for Ms Cullen's rather low-key comments to her membership.

Linked to that is the second negotiating point – did the constant repetition in the media of 19% and 5% above inflation start to crystallise an expectation in the minds of the membership of the RCN that this, or something close, might have been achievable? Did the climbdown from an unrealistic 19% to a negotiated 5% plus lump sum not meet the expectations of the RCN members who had expected a lot more? Moreover, did they expect a lot more because their leadership failed to manage their expectations about what was realistically achievable and to sell the deal as positively as you might think UNISON tried to do?

I don't know the answers to these questions, but I can tell you this with considerable confidence: wildly incredible proposals are never met in reality – indeed, they are sometimes not even given the courtesy of a response. Moreover, if you make a wildly unrealistic proposal and you keep repeating it and offering your justification for it, then you risk the possibility that you and others may believe it is achievable when it manifestly is not and the bump when you fall back to reality is so hard to bear that staying in the realms of fantasy may be preferable. Managing expectations about the achievability and the realism of a desired outcome is key to successful negotiating – failure to do it can cause a time-consuming and frustrating deadlock.

I am sympathetic to the issues of pay for those who work in the front line of the Health Service – some of whom I know as friends. It is the tactics which I question. If I were to offer advice in addition to what I have noted here about realism and expectation management, it would be to continue the initiative and to use time as a factor in the negotiation – make a proposal which uses time – probably a number of years – to keep the issues current and to rectify what has no doubt taken years to arrive at.

## Tell me why...
### Horace McDonald, 16th February 2023

Having become empty nesters when both our grown-up children left home in the middle of 2022, my wife and I are remodelling the house for different needs, which is something we've always enjoyed. We've replanned how we are going to use the kids' bedrooms and some of our furniture is now redundant. We'd inherited a rather unusual, but very useful, single bed from my mother-in-law, which had another single bed nested underneath it that could be wheeled out to turn it into a double. The lower bed needed to be managed with some caution, as there was no mechanism for locking the spring-loaded legs, and I'd suffered more than once when one of the legs shot out at me whilst manoeuvring it.

We'd been through a gamut of options of how to get rid of the bed and the two (nearly new) mattresses, including The British Heart Foundation (who'd refused to take a table some years ago because it wasn't in pristine condition); the local council who take stuff away for a fee; or selling it via the Nextdoor app. However, we were both keen for it to go to someone of real need and we preferred to give it away, which is what my wife's parents would have wanted.

So, I ended up posting on Freecycle. The unusual thing about Freecycle is that it doesn't work via an app, so having posted the bed on the site at midday, I'd expected to receive a bunch of texts, but it wasn't until I checked my 'partially hidden' emails later in the afternoon that I saw the many responses. My first instinct was to give the bed to the first respondent but thought best to read all eight emails. Most of the responses were fairly perfunctory, but one, from Vera, caught my eye. She explained that they couldn't afford to buy a new bed – bingo – and ended their message with 'Please let me know!' twice. A clear example of the power of persuasion in resolving the conflict about who I was going to give the bed to. On calling Vera, it became obvious to me that she had no access to transport, so knowing that van rental prices are very high in our area, I offered to deliver the bed (on the proviso that I could get it in the car).

Whilst this was not a negotiation, Vera employed a tactic akin to an **Opening Statement**, which we consider vital at the start of a negotiation where each party outlines their objectives, how they see them developing and may use it to outline areas of flexibility and in some cases inflexibility or no-go areas. In her email, Vera let me know how much she wanted the bed (not always appropriate in a negotiation), that she could take immediate delivery of it and where she lived (less than two miles away).

The good news is that the dismantled bed just about fitted into the car (helped by me closing the hatch by sitting on it) and was delivered to an incredibly grateful Vera and her partner to their housing estate on Sunday afternoon. To round up this little tale, she kindly gave me a box of what I assume to be sweets from her country of origin, which turned out to be marzipan – my wife's favourite and a gift that always appeared in her stocking as a child! Her parents would have been doubly pleased.

# Who goes first?
*Stephen White, 31st August 2023*

The single most common dilemma facing negotiators is 'who goes first?'. I know this because it is the most debated issue when we discuss proposal-making with Scotwork participants. The default position of most Northern Europeans and

North Americans is to hold back – let the other side pitch first. That way they might propose something even better for me than I was expecting. And if they don't, nothing is lost.

That is wrong, for two reasons. Firstly, because the probability of their proposal being unexpectedly better for you than the one you were going to pitch is vanishingly small. And secondly, because any proposal they make, as long as it is reasonable, is a powerful tool. It gains the ascendancy; it structures the geography of the deal. The counterparty has to overwhelm it to gain traction. And if the counterparty is you, be prepared for an uphill struggle to get back to where you wanted to be.

So our standard advice is – at the appropriate time to make a proposal, *go first*.

Except that sometimes standard advice is wrong. Here is an example.

My internet contract expired 18 months ago. The provider then pushed up the monthly 'out of contract' price from £44 to £50, and then a few weeks ago to £62. I was being taken for a can't-be-bothered-to-change mug. They should have been ashamed of themselves for taking advantage. In fact, eventually they were – they wrote to me to say there was a better deal available for loyal customers at £52.

On their website, the same deal was available to new subscribers at £32.50. That got me cross. I went on to live chat, expecting a battle.

Having established my credentials 'Kirsten' at their end asked me what my problem was. I replied that I wanted a better deal than £62 if I was going to renew my contract, and that I knew from their website that new subscribers got to pay £32.50, which I proposed should apply to me as well.

Kirsten stopped typing. Perhaps she had gone to make a cup of tea. I went to make a cup of tea.

When I got back to my screen Kirsten was typing again. She regretted that she couldn't offer me a rate of £32.50. However, she could offer me a rate of £32. Would that be OK?

I stopped typing. Was she playing with me? Were we in some sort of Monty Pythonesque world where I would complain that wasn't good enough, and reverse-negotiate the price up to £33? Or would she recognise her mistake – sorry, £32 was a mistype, I meant £52??

I changed the subject and asked if there were any newer router models which might come my way free of charge? No, I was up to date. I took the £32 deal.

I still don't understand it – perhaps Kirsten was an AI robot badly programmed. Perhaps it was a mistype but she was too embarrassed to admit it. Go figure. I am unexpectedly happy.

# A strategy in need of surgery?
## David Bannister, 12th September 2024

In the last few weeks, general practitioners (GPs) in the UK have announced what they describe as 'collective action'. For the first time in 60 years, GPs have adopted an approach involving restricting their work to achieve their objective of better pay and funding. This action is at the discretion of individual GP practices and was backed by a huge majority in a ballot. The last government offered them a 1.9% funding increase for this year, which the BMA (the doctors' union) considers inadequate and has now demanded 11%. The new Health Secretary, Wes Streeting, has made sympathetic noises and spoken of his desire to build a new partnership with GPs. Streeting has backed a recommended above-inflation 6% pay increase for GPs and their teams – a 4.1% uplift to GP contract funding on top of the 1.9% rise.

This dispute is set against the background of the resolution, shortly after the new government came into office, of the junior doctors' long-running dispute with a 22% unconditional two-year deal which is yet to be accepted. Also, a two-year dispute with train drivers has recently been the subject of another unconditional 15% three-year offer, which is being recommended for acceptance. It could be the case that the GPs reflect on the government's approach and the recent public sector pay award of just over 5% accompanied by the Chancellor's statement that it is 'cheaper than strikes' and decide that pressure works so why not apply it?

When you negotiate, your power will emanate from having the ability to inflict damage by doing something your counterparty doesn't want you to do – strike or impose restrictions or unfavourable conditions or even end a relationship – or from your ability to empower both parties to achieve something they want. Right now, I see Streeting as being on the back foot with the GPs – they are exerting pressure on the NHS and him and his concession to the junior doctors does not serve him well as a tactical precedent. The approach of the GPs is understandable because it has been successful for others. However, with a new government and the virtual certainty that they will be in office for at least the next five years, the Health Secretary has a strategic opportunity. He could paint a long-term vision of an NHS that the GPs would support and he could release funding and pay increases as the vision is achieved within an agreed timescale. That approach may need some financial priming now to get buy-in but if the ultimate objective and the route to it and changes needed are agreed as part of the deal then he has an opportunity to define and build the partnership he has spoken of. Yet more unilateral concessions will, I predict, reinforce the current precedent and lead to yet more pressure and action in the public sector.

This may be an opportunity to change the dynamic of relationships in the NHS and move from the image of perpetually aggrieved staff, industrial action and budgetary restrictions to a government and staff agreeing a future, knowing what it will cost the parties in terms of finance and working practices and committing to work towards it. Consensus generally can achieve more than conflict – building a shared vision will be the critical part but let us hope that, with the will to achieve, it can be done.

## Proposals that take the risk
*Ellis Croft, 27th October 2022*

As keen students of all things negotiation related (oh, go on then: we're nerds), a group of us at Scotwork regularly discuss blog topics and what's going on around us. Responding to my suggestion to write about the 'mini' budget sitting at the base of the volcano that recently erupted underneath the Truss government, a colleague (wiser, more experienced and definitely smarter than me) pointed out that by the time we published a blog about this subject, we'd have a new PM, events would have moved on and 'it may as well have been written by Homer'. I don't think he meant Simpson. I do think, however, that it's true – and it encapsulates one of the lessons we can draw from what the 'mini' budget might tell us about our own negotiations.

One of the perennial topics of debate with participants on our courses revolves around whether pitching a proposal may be most effective. The debate tends to coalesce around a spectrum we can call 'ambitious' – where one end is tempered by realism and credibility, and the other by moving the goalposts by being more extreme. Our advice is that – for the most part – a realistic proposal will be in your best interests. In the sense that the 'mini' budget was a series of fiscal measures yet to be enacted; it was a proposal.

If we're going to measure that proposal on our spectrum of ambition, then the following evidence could have helped: the measures were estimated by the *Financial Times* to add up to a cost of £45bn; when announced, funding the cost was not included; the Office of Budget Responsibility (put in place by the Coalition government ten years ago) were not given the necessary time to comment on the proposed measures, and as a result the markets saw severe and negative responses. It would, I think, be fair to characterise the package of measures as being at the extreme end of the spectrum.

One risk of 'going big' when we make an ask is the potential reaction from the other party in the negotiation. In this instance, the market response demonstrated the risk that the response may make matters worse and act against your best interests. Another risk inherent in extreme proposals is that they can engender equally extreme counter-proposals – in this instance, the sacking of both the then-Chancellor and then-PM.

The risks associated with extremely ambitious proposals can be related to the uncertainty principle. If nobody really knows what a fair, accurate or appropriate price looks like (for example, with an entirely new product or market) then being extremely ambitious may result in other parties moving their goalposts towards you. The simple truth is that for most of us, the majority of our negotiations take place with people who do know their markets and other data that will inform their estimate as to how realistic a proposal may be – there will still be a degree of uncertainty, for sure, but it will narrow. And as we saw with the short-lived government of Liz Truss, getting it wrong can have unforeseen consequences – becoming a historical footnote worthy of Homer being one of the more sobering.

## The meaning of lie
*Ellis Croft, 22nd June 2023*

The information we have to process – in life and in negotiations – can prove frequently challenging. This is particularly the case where ambiguity intrudes. Occasionally, poor outcomes may arise from acting in good faith on information that later turns out to have been inaccurate. Sometimes this may be due to a simple, unintentional mistake – and after ascertaining whether we can do anything to avoid similar errors in future, we move on. Sometimes, however, it can be more nuanced. What if we have been misled, and worse, deliberately so?

Most of us would accept that a lie is characterised by being both false and deliberate. Negotiators may be wearily familiar with some of the navigational perils that distortion can present. Frequently, there can be more to it than that and truth can be equally misleading. Consider the recent defenestration of former UK Prime Minister Boris Johnson at the hands of his former parliamentary colleagues. Whatever you think of him, Johnson is a master of manipulating language. It became apparent – as a result of the police investigation and subsequent fines – that the assurance Johnson offered in Parliament in December 2021 that 'the rules were followed at all times' was inaccurate. Interestingly, it was precise language. Compare and contrast to the imprecision of the second part of the same statement: 'I have been repeatedly assured since these allegations emerged that there was no party and that no Covid rules were broken.' This may well be accurate, but as we have no idea who the assurances came from – Larry the Downing Street cat, perhaps – there is scope for interpretation here absent from the absolutism of the first statement. So we can be precise and inaccurate, and accurate but imprecise – both might be seen as misleading, but in different ways.

The ability to use imprecision combined with accuracy to dissemble in a way which evades accusations of deliberate deception is a minefield for negotiators. If when asked for an increase by a supplier citing inflationary pressures and other external factors as the driving forces, you naturally respond by querying the amount; the response '8% would cover it' can be interpreted as, well, 8%. However, the phrasing should send a signal to the seasoned negotiator. It may well be accurate – but then so might 7%, or 6%, or less. We should be alert to imprecision and probe accordingly, all the while being aware that sometimes imprecision is simply a product of reluctance to be direct – and that there may be no attempt to conceal an alternative at all. Equally, we should be careful about any propensity we may have to exploit imprecision in our own interests – in the majority of commercial situations, the probability of any gap being exposed over time is high. On that basis weighing up the risk of how that might land versus the likely incremental gain would suggest that it's most often in our own interests to avoid taking advantage through imprecise use of language or data. And if we find ourselves tempted, consider the vote that carried the cross-party committee's findings in the parliamentary division – of Conservative MPs, a mere seven voted in Johnson's support and 118 found that he deliberately and recklessly misled the House. And the remaining 200+? They had better things to be doing, apparently… Johnson's reputation for having a cavalier attitude towards being truthful isn't new, and it might have taken him 30 years or more to finally burn through whatever was left of the mitigating goodwill he generated with his charisma, but it certainly is a warning to the curious when it comes to telling lies for advantage.

# Pholly

*Stephen White, 8th June 2023*

'If the facts don't fit the theory change the facts' is a quote often attributed to Einstein, although it appears nowhere in his published works. Unsurprisingly so, because it is unhelpful nonsense, something Einstein did not specialise in. Unfortunately, it is a concept that is becoming more and more common, as we have seen over the last few days with the saga of Philip Schofield and his second-line casualty Holly Willoughby.

I won't go over the well-trodden ground – unless you are a hermit you know how the story of his demise unfolded.

But I couldn't help but notice the similarity of his story with another story; the lamentable handling by Dorset police of the tragic loss of two young people in a swimming incident in Bournemouth. The similarity is that of invention, suppression and manipulation of facts in both cases that encouraged speculative theories which the media would like to have us believe; mainly sensationalist and always in the pursuit of sales rather than truth. Thrilling – maybe. Helpful – absolutely not.

The link is silence. Phil lied to his bosses and his wife about the affair, and apparently also lied to Holly, and in the whirlwind of disbelief that followed was silent about the truth for much too long. This created the space for rumour-mongering on a massive scale. Holly went on an extended holiday when the news broke, and was essentially silent for two weeks, allowing the newspapers and social media to invent a range of her emotions. In Bournemouth, the early police statements about the cause of the tragedy were opaque and unhelpful except to those who wanted to indulge in wild imaginings of the cause. I am not a conspiracy theorist but I will admit to watching the news about the swimming disaster and wondering what the cause could possibly have been if it was not contact with a jet-ski, or interference from a ferry boat, or jumping off the pier. When the obvious is ruled out (which is what the police statements did) and there is silence about what was more likely, fanciful invention is all that is left. All that was necessary was an admission that there was no obvious cause, but it was most likely to have been a sudden rip tide and that inquiries were proceeding.

For negotiators, the faux cliché attributed to Einstein morphs into 'if the facts don't fit the argument, change the facts', which is also unhelpful nonsense. Timing in a negotiation is always key – when to reveal a new piece of information or make a proposal or shift ground. Negotiators tend to procrastinate; holding back so as to see what might happen from the other side. Often that decision is undermined by pressure from the other side and if that pressure provokes a lie then negotiators find themselves on a slippery slope. Most commonly this occurs when an unrealistic proposal is defended by an untruthful assertion (your competitor's price is 20% lower than yours). Requests for substantiation are met with – you guessed it – either bluster or silence.

Control of the facts is a key skill. Usually disclosure of what you want – and which facts lead you to believe that to be tenable – is always best put up earlier rather than later, denying the opportunity for speculation about your position. The no-no is more likely to be focussing on the emotional issues – how you feel and what the conflict is doing to your mental health. Disclosing how *badly* you need what you are asking for, either verbally or by your body language, is also counterproductive and not recommended.

The combined contents of Phil's BBC interview with Amol Rajan, Holly's emotional statement when she returned to ITV's *This Morning*, and the early statements from Dorset police, prove the point.

# CHAPTER 5

# PACKAGING TO CREATE MORE VALUE

If your proposal is not acceptable to the other party, it is because it either does not address their needs and excites their inhibitions or because it is simply not enough. If it is the former, then it is a packaging issue, if it is the latter, it is a bargaining issue. If you have opened realistically, then very often it is possible to reach a deal without making any further concessions. In order to do so you must first identify the **inhibitions** and the **interests** and address the package to them. If you adopt a **competitive** stance then it is less likely that you will be told about the inhibitions and interests than if you adopt a **cooperative** stance.

*Proposals are solutions to needs*:

- Before you begin to respond to a proposal attempt to identify the need.
- There may be another solution to the problem that involves a lower cost.

*Think creatively about the variables*:

- The first item on any list of variables is **time**.

It is vitally important to *value your concessions in the other party's terms* – what is it worth to the other party? We distinguish responses to negotiations along these lines that we describe as being 'Sumo' or 'Judo'. In Sumo, when receiving a proposal, there can be a tendency for the receiving party to make their proposal with no consideration to the proposal received; think of it like two Sumo wrestlers going at one another aggressively with their proposals, which, if not contained, move the negotiation back to the **Argue** step and be counterproductive. Judo, by contrast, is subtler, as it requires each fighter to understand what the other fighter is trying to do, work with it and use it to their advantage.

# It's a man's world?...
## Ann Parr, 30th March 2023
### Negotiating as a woman: Navigating gender stereotypes

A number of years ago, I spent some time working in a senior sales role overseas for a global FMCG business. When I walked into the meeting room for the briefing on our annual sales strategy, you could have heard a pin drop. I was young (and foreign) but I don't believe it was either of these elements that caused the unease. In a room filled entirely with men, I firmly believe the real issue was that I was female.

That was over 20 years ago and in the words of Bob Dylan 'Times They Are A-Changing' but nevertheless I still hear regular tales in the classroom from some of the women we teach about the challenges they face in dealing with gender stereotypes. I hear comments like 'I get talked down to, told I'm too nice, too emotional' and occasionally 'they won't even talk business with me when my older, male colleague is around'. Thankfully this 'time machine' of attitudes from the 1950s is not as common as it was then, but I still hear it and it still exists.

One of the most common stereotypes is that women are less assertive than men. I can't tell you how many times I've heard the phrase 'she's too nice' used to describe a female negotiator. But here's the thing: being nice is not a weakness. In fact, it can be a strength when combined with assertiveness. If nice is another word for collaborative or cooperative then, for a negotiator, that can frankly be turned into a superpower. Collaborative negotiators are more likely to really listen to the other party and thereby get a genuine understanding of their objectives, issues, concerns and constraints as well as picking up nuances of language that might suggest areas of flexibility. That information, if used constructively, can be turned into a proposal that addresses the needs of both parties and therefore has a likely chance of success.

Collaborative negotiators are more likely to make people feel comfortable sharing information with them, thereby recognising packaging opportunities when they present themselves. This is invaluable for a negotiator since it often enables a proposal to be simply reshaped rather than increased to get it over the line.

Another stereotype that we face is the idea that women are too emotional and irrational to be effective negotiators… back to that time machine again! Effective preparation with clarity of objectives enables a focus on the issues, though emotion can be a powerful tool in negotiation if used wisely.

As a female negotiator, I've always found two things incredibly useful if faced with navigating the stereotype minefield. Being effectively prepared is crucial. If we're talking superpowers, great preparation is up there in terms of building confidence to deal with whatever challenges the negotiation brings. The second is making proposals. There's nothing like effective proposals to keep the focus on making progress with the issues and taking focus away from less helpful attitudes or behaviour.

As women, we need to support each other and learn from one another. I have learned from some amazing women (and men) in my career and it can be helpful to seek out someone who has faced similar challenges for guidance and support.

And finally, let's not forget that negotiating as a woman is not just an individual challenge, but a systemic one as well. It's important to advocate for systemic changes that promote gender equality and create a more level playing field for all negotiators, regardless of gender.

# When is the price the *price*?
## Horace McDonald, 5th September 2024

Undoubtedly, the biggest news of last week was the announcement of Oasis reforming to play a number of shows in the UK (which will undoubtedly spread across the globe). The level of both positive and negative feedback to this announcement has been interesting. For the diehard fans, who represent a broader span of age groups than you might think, it is something akin to the second coming. Whilst the band fell apart in 2009, they have remained in the public eye due to the much-reported animosity between the two key members, Noel and Liam Gallagher. The fact that they have since formed separately successful bands in their own right – and that they would be unable to resist the millions they would earn from the tour – has kept them in the headlines.

Oasis's first album, *Definitely Maybe*, was released on 29 August 1994, the week before I joined EMI Records, and at the time it was the fastest-selling debut album in the UK. They undoubtedly had a huge impact on society and popular culture with their swagger, look and songwriting in a world of only 30 years ago. Their second album, *Be Here Now*, became the fifth biggest-selling album in chart history. To some degree this was driven by the rivalry generated by the British press when they released the single 'Roll with It' on the same day as a rival band at the time, Blur, released the single 'Country House', who won the battle and who were signed to an EMI label. Since those heady days, the music industry has been on a roller-coaster ride with the virtual extinction of physical products (vinyl is very small, really) and the lack of attention given to chart and chart positions.

As well as through streaming, technology has had a huge impact on touring and ticket prices. It never ceases to amaze me how expensive gig tickets have become and that's even before the scammers have scalped a quantity for the secondary ticket market. A good friend of ours spent £1,000 per ticket for his partner and daughter to see Taylor Swift at Wembley! It is also worth noting that whilst the column inches are taken up with stories of excessive pricing, technology has made it much easier for promoters and theatres to make late tickets available at lower prices, so it's not all doom and gloom, but it's certainly not in balance.

The tickets for Oasis's shows have been put on sale almost a year in advance. This and the introduction of 'dynamic pricing' (introduced by Ticketmaster in 2022), has meant that fans have waited in online ticketing queues for hours at a time and watched the prices balloon, with reports that 'Platinum' tickets were over £6,000. This has led to calls for the whole ticketing system to be reviewed. It will be interesting to see how many shows the band end up playing. In 1996, the band played two shows at Knebworth to 250,000 people and Noel Gallagher revealed in a later documentary that they had sufficient demand for seven; there was no secondary ticketing in those days!

As a negotiator, on the relatively rare instance where I see an artist live, my first port of call is to assess the *intend* price (the price has been set by the promoter) and then a *limit* beyond which I won't pay if I have to use the secondary market or I'm subject to dynamic pricing. The latest example of this was Janet Jackson at the O2: *intend* £85, *limit* £150, and by the time I made up my mind, the prices had gone to over £250. There is genuinely NO artist I would pay that money for, regardless of how much money the artist needs to pay for their latest divorce.

## 'Tis a season to be (not so) jolly
*Horace McDonald, 16th December 2022*

Having emerged from a very challenging two years, I'm sure that many of you had high hopes that 2022 would be much better and that life would return to what we considered to be normal. The impact of the vaccination programme in many countries meant that we could meet, travel, entertain and work without restriction. Whilst the impacts of the pandemic were extremely stark, certain changes in working practices and the use of technology would continue to make many people's everyday lives easier.

As we approach the end of 2022, different challenges have emerged, which have had very significant impacts and appear to show little sign of abating in the short-term. At around the point where it was possible to feel that the worst of the pandemic was behind us, Russia invaded Ukraine which has significantly raised tensions between the 'democratic' and communist countries, causing huge devastation across vast swathes of Ukraine. It has resulted in thousands of deaths on both sides, as well as triggering a major supply-side crisis that has helped to fuel significant increases in the rate of inflation, which in turn have resulted in interest rate rises.

In the UK, we have experienced a triple whammy due to the impacts of Brexit. Whilst our current Prime Minister, Rishi Sunak, is still extolling the virtues of the UK leaving the EU, the European Commission predicts the reduction in GDP will be about 2.25% in 2022, which on top of the economic impacts of high inflation and higher interest rates will mean that the UK will suffer more than any major economy in Europe.

Rampant inflation after a long period of near-zero inflation and very low interest rates has hit everyone, in particular public sector workers, whose employer's decisions are heavily influenced by the government. A significant number of these employees are union members, who have sought double-digit pay increases from employers whose masters are advocating wage restraint as a means of trying to control inflation. This incendiary cocktail has resulted in workers in the rail, postal, airport and health industries staging or announcing strikes in late 2022. Arguably the most significant being 100,000 nurses going on strike in England alone for the first time in their history.

Pat Cullen, the leader of the nurses' union, has accused the Health Secretary, Steve Barclay, of 'bullyboy' tactics, being unwilling to negotiate with her as she is a woman representing a largely female workforce and has also claimed that the government was displaying 'particularly macho' behaviour towards the Royal College of Nursing (RCN). Cullen cites a recent meeting being publicised by Barclay's team, despite it being private, being made to wait before it and Barclay abruptly exiting the meeting rather than engaging in dialogue. It is also worth noting that claims were made about the lack of female representation in Sunak's cabinet, particularly in the most senior positions.

Much has been written in the past about women being more adept at more collaborative negotiation, which requires effective preparation, a willingness to engage in constructive dialogue and ensuring the delivery of realistic proposals. The latter is moot, as the RCN had asked for a 5% above inflation. However, as a means of driving the process forward, they have offered to withdraw the 5% increment if the Health Secretary abandoned his refusal for meaningful talks.

This is set against a backdrop of huge waiting lists, partly due to a huge shortage of nurses, and a significant level of public sympathy, which is a worry for the government.

So, as we look towards 2023, I have to be optimistic that the plethora of strikes amongst our public services (and beyond) are resolved quickly. As I write this, the nurses are threatening to step up strikes unless pay is improved and on a more positive note, the Transport Salaried Staffs Association (the second largest union behind the RMT (Rail, Maritime and Transport Workers Union)) have voted to accept an improved pay deal in a referendum.

A glimmer of good news in a challenging year, where the need to negotiate as a means of resolving conflict is as relevant as ever.

## 'Ave yer done?

### David Bannister, 22nd August 2024

I live close to the route of the LNER (London North Eastern Railway) link to London from Scotland along the East Coast. The franchise previously held by Virgin was nationalised four years ago. Like other rail lines, it has been in a long-running dispute over pay by the unions – RMT and ASLEF (the train drivers' union) who have called intermittent strikes to exert pressure. The previous government made offers of settlement but they were attached to conditions that were an attempt to get rid of some of the more archaic work practices that had been agreed over the years. For example, if a manager speaks to a train driver while the driver is having a break, the driver can start his break again from the beginning – even if the manager just says 'Hello'. The unions resisted any change.

The new Transport Secretary, Louise Haigh, has offered ASLEF, which represents the train drivers, a three-year 15% overall settlement with no conditions attached to it. ASLEF has recommended acceptance. Haigh suggested that the cost of settling was less than the cost of the dispute. Let me examine that.

First of all, it took less than a day before the leader of the RMT – the union representing most of the other rail workers – made it clear that anything less than an equal settlement would not be accepted. Precedent is becoming an easily used tactic in the public sector amongst a workforce including doctors, teachers and civil servants all of whom have been offered unconditional above-inflation increases in pay in the last few weeks.

Next, ASLEF announced a prolonged weekend work to rule on LNER as it said that there had been a breakdown in agreements between the union and the rail operator. This is a dispute apparently linked to bonuses paid to management for driving trains during the ASLEF strike amongst other things. Morale is said by the union to be 'in the gutter' amongst its members who will earn £69,000 a year for a four-day, 35-hour week.

What can negotiators learn from this?

First, anyone who has been on a Scotwork course will always remember the concept of the 'elk steak' – the concession made without conditions. They will also remember that this kind of open-handed generosity will rarely, if ever, be met with gratitude. It is likely to lead to requests for more of the same. It remains to be seen if the deals offered to junior doctors, civil servants and train drivers create more demand elsewhere when they might have been linked to changes in working practices in return for settlements. My prediction is that the tactic of conceding demands because it is cheaper than having industrial action will simply encourage more demands and more threats of action – 'if they get something for nothing, we want it too' as the RMT have said. However it works out, it is unlikely to be the cheap option.

Second, it is a very good practice when you negotiate to ensure that all issues are on the table and that, wherever possible, they are linked and resolved together. Using a simple expression like 'is that everything that we need to resolve between us' should flush out issues that have not emerged or are being held back to exert further pressure in the end game when the prospect of abandoning all the good work to get a consensus can, and often does, lead to further, usually unconditional, concessions. In Yorkshire where I am from, we say ''Ave yer done?'. The lesson here, of course, is always to have a wish list to counter the tactic.

Government ministries littered with elk steaks and representatives getting to the end of negotiations and saying, like the fictional detective, Columbo, 'just one more thing' does not bode well for future negotiations.

## You want it when????
*Stephen White, 26th January 2023*

After Christmas and New Year, we needed a break. Hosting four children and five grandchildren for two weeks is great fun, very uplifting but exhausting. That is the price that comes with living by the seaside – even in a wet and windy winter, there is a magical attraction. But when they all went home we felt we needed some R&R (rest and recuperation) ourselves.

We decided on a couple of days in Cornwall, focussing on the Eden Project and the Tate in St Ives. Where to stay? One of the 'restaurants with rooms' had space, so we booked online. An hour or so later I got a call from the receptionist.

'We have a special January offer,' she said. ' Lunch for two in the restaurant, glass of champagne, welcome gift, afternoon tea, all for only £xxx'. It was an actual bargain – about half the price of a meal for two in the restaurant alone.

I said that sounded excellent, but we were committed at lunchtime on both days at Eden and St Ives. Could we do dinner instead? No – she was adamant – this was a lunchtime offer only. I appealed to her better nature. She agreed to ask a supervisor and get back to me.

In the meantime, I did a bit of research. The restaurant was open for dinner from 5.30pm, and on one of the two nights, there was plenty of early evening availability.

The following day she called back. 'Sorry, but this is a lunchtime-only offer.'

'What if we agreed to have a very late lunch?' I asked. 'Would the offer still be available?' 'How late were you thinking?' she said. 'About 5.30,' I said. There was a pause. 'I'll see if we can accommodate you for a late lunch,' she said. 'Would 5.30 be OK?'

It's on Thursday this week. I'll let you know how the meal was.

# Another fine mess!
*Alan Smith, 18th May 2023*

Ever found yourself in that nightmare scenario when you are in front of another party in a negotiation and the partner you have taken with you to the meeting seems to have gone off track, starts revealing new information, giving in on things you had both agreed before the negotiation, being conciliatory when they should have been tough or tough when they should have been conciliatory?

Even worse, the other side have picked up on this and have started to focus on your colleague, even though you had agreed to lead the negotiation?

A lot of this can be solved through being thoroughly prepared for the negotiation and having a clear plan, but it can be tough in the real world when your partner (who may even be your boss!) starts to go rogue.

If you have seen the fantastic movie, *Stan and Ollie*, you can see just how easy it can be to go off track, and how in the case of Laurel and Hardy it can set the tone for the rest of your life.

Stan Laurel and Oliver Hardy were at the height of their powers, making successful films for the legendary producer Hal Roach. Roach was born in 1892 in New York. After a tough life working as a mule skinner, wrangler and gold prospector, among other things, he wound up in Hollywood and began picking up jobs as an extra in comedies. By all accounts, including his own, he was a terrible actor, but he saw a future in the movie business and in producing movies, particularly comedies.

His relationship as the producer for Laurel and Hardy was very much on his terms. He paid the two stars (stars as they would be today) a salary which meant that despite their success they remained relatively poor, taking no share of the box office, which frankly is how most successful actors today make the big money through acquiring executive producer status, but was pretty rare in those days.

The other clever move was to keep Laurel and Hardy on separate and unsynchronised contracts. When Laurel's contract came up for renewal he and Hardy agreed to ask for changes which Roach refused. Hardy then did not stick to their plan and carried on making films for Roche without Laurel, which partly caused the pair to fall out of favour and both to lose out.

On screen, Hardy was the father figure to the more innocent Laurel but off-screen their personalities were very different, with Laurel being the more serious professional. While Hardy was happy leaving his work behind when he left the set to go gambling or play golf, Laurel was a workaholic, refining scripts and film-takes long into the night.

These differences did not help them as a team and Roach seemed to be able to pull them apart despite their obvious respect, admiration and indeed love for each other.

What's the answer to these challenges? Well, if you find yourself unable to control your colleague despite all the preparation and practice you can afford, and that taking time out during the meeting to get it back on track still doesn't work, then my advice is to not take them with you. Take someone else or just do it yourself with their authority.

For Hardy, maybe he would have been able to maintain the partnership with Laurel more profitably by breaking it for the negotiation. It certainly got them into a 'fine mess' by them doing it together.

## The hair stays

*Tom Feinson, 2nd November 2023*

'We've already established what you are – now we are just haggling over the price.' This story is so well known that I don't need to describe the full scenario – but do you know who said it?

Variously attributed to George Bernard Shaw, Winston Churchill, Groucho Marx, Mark Twain, W.C. Fields and the list goes on; in truth, no one really knows its etymology. The likelihood is it began life as a joke, which was subsequently retold using various famous characters.

The interesting question it raises for me from a negotiator's perspective is the idea that everyone has their price and ultimately it's us who choose when we agree to be bought. Is it true that regardless of our principles we can be influenced or motivated to do something different if an appropriate financial reward is offered?

Enter stage left, Gifton Noel-Williams, ex-Premier League player and owner of one of the truly great footballers' names. He caught my attention this week with this statement: 'If I don't become a manager because of my hair that's ok. It's hard to become a football manager, and statistically, the odds are against a black player becoming a manager. Only 4.4% of manager-related roles are held by black players, despite them representing 43% of players.'

Rationally, you might argue that cutting your hair is a pretty small price to pay for getting the job you want, especially if you have as little as I have. However, we are all differently shaped by our experiences, beliefs, values and sense of right and wrong. Gifton started growing his hair out of respect for his uncle, a Rastafarian, who was going through cancer and losing his own hair. So, the hair is staying.

Whilst I am slightly in awe of this principled stance, the point here is not about right or wrong but about how we all see the world differently and how all perspectives are equally valid. So, does everyone have their price? I don't think so – I can't see Gifton change his principled position based on financial reward. Me, on the other hand?

It's important as a negotiator to understand whether an issue is a point of price or principle to the other party. One way to do this is to make proposals both specific and vague, for example, a seller may say to a buyer 'If you give me 100% of your business I might be prepared to reduce my price.' In this situation the seller is making a specific demand and a vague concession, the important part is the response. If the buyer looks to explore the size of the discount it would indicate that the issue is a point of price. If, however, the response is along the lines of strategically managing the supply chain to ensure availability and competition the issue is more likely a point of principle.

## Drastic discounts or deception...
*Siobhan Bermingham, 16th November 2023*

As Black Friday fast approaches the hum of excitement is building, murmurs of killer deals and discussions about treating oneself to items you might otherwise never consider buying. Is this due to the 'huge discounts' or is it the illusion of the limited time offer and FOMO (fear of missing out)?

In recent years, more and more people have become savvy to the false perception created around discounts and Black Friday – a large percentage of companies intentionally inflate prices ahead of time to enable them to slash down their prices for Black Friday and still maintain their profit margins. As much as this tactic has worked for a period, more and more people are becoming disillusioned by the Black Friday pricing games.

When it comes to negotiation, especially with long-term partners, there is certainly a risk to giving drastic discounts.

Firstly, it can then set a precedent for future negotiations having large discounts, and secondly, the party receiving the discount may become uncomfortable with the deal and wonder whether there is still more money/margin on the table, resulting in negotiations being opened up again. Far from the outpouring of thanks you may have expected for your 'goodwill' pricing slash.

When negotiating it's important to structure the expectations of the other party. Remember that giving in too easily sets a precedent for future negotiations. Rather than handing out huge discounts, move modestly and always trade any shift in pricing for a concession from the other party or the closing of the deal.

Become a creative negotiator – think beyond price and volume. Much like a sofa during Black Friday, deals don't have to only be drastically discounted in price – it could instead be packaged into a deal that's more appealing than the sofa on its own, for example, a package deal of two sofas, a matching footstool and optional furnishing accessories. Always find out, what is the gap to close this deal? Is there a price issue – in which case work on bargaining and move modestly. Or is it a shape issue – in which case keep the overall value the same but repackage how it is presented/shaped.

As for me, I'll still take a sceptical, quick glance at the online 'discounts' this Black Friday. After all, maybe I'll find a justifiable excuse to purchase an impressive gadget I know deep down I will hardly use.

## CHAPTER 6

# BARGAIN TO CREATE MORE VALUE

At Scotwork, we passionately believe that any proposal you make should be one that you think the other party can accept. In making one, you should always be ready for a counterproposal, which is when the bargaining process typically starts. However, bargaining can take place at any stage of the negotiation; for information, for concessions, for signals, for time and for the deal itself (see **Close** step). In the **Proposal** stage of the book, we have covered the disadvantages of making extreme proposals.

Bargaining takes place in a repositioning of variables and is underpinned by one of the most important principles in negotiation – ensure that you get something in return for any concession you make and by valuing your concessions in the other party's terms. Doing so ensures that the value created is maintained by (where possible) trading low-cost items (concessions) for items of high value. Hence, if they ask for more of something, you need to make a proposal that ensures you get (more) value back in return.

How you articulate any bargaining proposal is critical, in that you state the condition before the offer, so by way of example, at the end of dinner with one of your children, rather than say:

'I will let you have ice cream as long as you eat your cabbage.'

It is better to say:

'If (and only if) you eat all your cabbage, then (and only then) will I let you have some ice cream.'

The latter makes a statement, avoids interruption and forces the other party to think of it as a trade-off.

## Price increases
### Tom Feinson, 9th March 2023

I recently received a letter from my broadband supplier (from now on known as supplier X) telling me that their prices were increasing, and changes were being made to services and pricing terms. To be specific the cost of my broadband was to go up by 40%. I rang supplier X and after selecting half a dozen options I got to the 'I'm thinking of leaving queue'. Whilst I waited an automated voice told me that my price increase had been cut by 50% for the next three months. Wow, if this is the discount I get for simply calling just imagine what I'll get if I actually speak to someone. After a surprisingly short wait that happened and I explained my situation, they scuttled off to see what they could do and within ten minutes they came back and offered to give me a discount that matched the price increase for the rest of the term of my contract.

I couldn't work out whether I was appalled or elated. Why would a sensible grown-up company go to the trouble of increasing prices to immediately discount them back? The answer can be found in the 'rule of thirds'. It is believed that when a price increase is imposed (the same works for cost-down initiatives) about one-third accept without complaint, one-third completely rejects and one-third look to negotiate. Therefore, even if you concede with one-third, overall you'll come out on top. Whilst there is a logic to this, the 'rule of thirds' is not absolute; anyone putting up prices can influence the ratios in their favour.

So, if you're looking to increase prices here are some tips to help maximise acceptance, minimise rejection and get the best value out of a negotiation.

It starts with clarity. Be specific about what you want, what your message is, where you have flexibility and where you don't.

Once you have identified what you want, ask for it and be specific. In this situation, I was told exactly how much my broadband would be going up. So far so good. However, supplier X let themselves down by making an extreme demand. Even in the current environment a 40% price increase is unrealistic and will be seen as an opening gambit that will be rejected. You will increase your chances of getting what you want if what you ask for is realistic.

I was also told when it was going to happen. This helps create a sense of urgency and removes the status quo as an option. Tell people when it's going to happen, give a reasonable lead time and implement it when you say you are going to.

If you are familiar with the cognitive bias 'loss aversion', you'll understand why supplier X took the opportunity to not only increase prices but also reduce the service and change contractual terms. If you have bad news share it all in one go rather than on a piecemeal basis.

Develop a simple repeatable message that intuitively makes sense and everyone delivers. Explain it in consumer terms, remind them of the value and demonstrate market acceptance. Supplier X devoted two lines out of two pages to explain the context and referred only to the 'quality of service you'd expect from us' to remind me of the value I was getting from them – lazy and generic. Neither the rationale nor the value message were ever spoken of again during my interactions with customer service.

Once you have made your pitch be prepared for pushback. Remember, even if a third are sufficiently apathetic to simply accept that leaves two-thirds to deal with, who will be looking to delay, diminish or dismiss and will employ a range of tactical devices to do so. The first and most widely used is flat-out refusal, computer says no, often allied with brinkmanship, threats of all the unpleasant things that will happen to you if you persist and hope that deters you. If it doesn't you are likely to face delaying tactics. Don't be surprised if you're asked to provide evidence to demonstrate the basis of the increase. This is often a ploy to lure you into what is essentially a filibuster where implementation of a price rise is delayed by drawing you into the minutiae of technical/procedural differences of opinion. Don't be deterred, stick to your guns and eventually they will recognise that you're not going away. At some point, you'll hear words to the effect of 'so what is it that you want?'.

Once you move into this phase you need to calculate how strongly you will hold the line. Key determinants are dependency and risk. In my interaction with supplier X, there was no effort to negotiate. It may well be that I would have accepted less and/or provided them more value for their concession. Therefore, it's in your interests to have identified trading variables that will create value for you/the other party that you can use to create value based on the initial proposal. Even if you conclude that ultimately you will have to concede don't signpost to the other party that it's likely to happen as you will encourage them to push back. At all points during my experience with supplier X the signals I received encouraged me to keep going and expect more.

Oh, and one last thing, be alert to this phrase, 'Oh, and one last thing'. It is rarely delivered by accident and is almost always a ploy to secure additional concessions in the end game.

## Cupid's arrows

*Ellis Croft, 9th February 2023*

Valentine's Day: for those of us lucky enough to be with somebody we love, it can be a source of renewal, affirmation, happiness – and, once in a while, stress and frustration usually, when trying to book that special table in the lovely little place we both decided we'd have to go back to...

If you'll forgive me for surgically removing the romance from Valentine's Day, there are perhaps a couple of key insights that a curious negotiator might think about in relation to their own deal making. Firstly – and perhaps most obviously – there's the rather expensive business of differential value. Is that bouquet *normally* that price? Does the set menu at our favourite haunt *usually* look quite so toppy? What possessed me to order the champagne instead of the prosecco?

For a myriad of reasons, many of us will be more than prepared to dig that little bit (or a lot) deeper into our pockets than usual come Valentine's Day. To a negotiator, it's a crucial skill to build in terms of recognising that differential value can improve the quality of our deals – all year round. Variables that we might find relatively easy and simple to concede (usually because they have little value to us) could have a far greater importance to the other party, and exploring that value – and trading against it – will unlock other value that we are more interested in.

Amplifying this is the other transferable variable Valentine's Day illustrates well: time. A dozen red roses on the 14th of February versus the 16th? It's fair to say that in most scenarios, there's a distance between them in terms of the likely reception. Of course, this also introduces no little pressure into the occasion – there's a fairly clear and immovable deadline here, after all. But creative negotiators will also think about time – does a buyer have the flexibility in their strategy to enable a purchase decision to benefit from the hockey-stick effect at the end of a supplier's financial quarter? Can a commercial negotiator use time to create scarcity while still allowing for the deal to be made? Time is both infinitely flexible and absolute – which end of that spectrum works in your best interests?

Having rather harshly de-romanticised the occasion, I'll leave the last words to Katharine Hepburn – they're my favourite on the subject. Quick caveat – try not to apply this advice to your negotiations! 'Love has nothing to do with what you are expecting to get – only with what you are expecting to give – which is everything.'

# Just plumb wrong!
## David Bannister, 27th July 2023

In my house, I had, until recently, a large copper tank that contained our hot water supply. Some years ago, I had a 'rainwater' shower installed – one of these wonderful things that cascade hot water over you in the morning as you brace yourself to face the day. This shower's appetite for hot water meant that I also had to have a special pump installed to deal with the relatively low water pressure in the house. A plumber installed the pump as part of the shower installation and all was well for more than two years until one day an anguished cry from the shower room told me that the pump was no longer working and it had chosen my wife to be the person to experience its failure. Undaunted, I dug out the warranty details – the pump was guaranteed for five years – and called the manufacturer. I was told that their engineer would visit to assess the pump and that it would be replaced provided that it had been 'installed in accordance with our instructions'. The visit would be free of charge unless the installation did not meet with the approval of the engineer when I would be charged £95 plus VAT of 20% and they would not replace the pump which cost £500.

A few days later their engineer, a man not notable for his cheery disposition, arrived and inspected the installation. He looked at the pump, the pipework, the storage tank and the header tank in the roof space grunting and muttering ominously. At the end of the inspection, he took a clipboard from his van and stood in the kitchen entering many ticks and crosses on a lengthy form (never a good omen in my view). He signed the form with a flourish and presented me with a carbon copy explaining that just about everything that could be wrong was wrong. He trotted me through all the errors saying that he would not install the replacement pump and I would be getting a bill.

I called my regular heating engineer and he came to see me. On his advice, we decided to bring forward a plan we had already discussed to have a new hot water system installed – it is called mains pressurised hot water. I don't understand it except to tell you that as I sit here writing this blog, there is a quarter of a ton of hot water in a tank above my head (I try not to think about it) but no pump is needed and it all works fine. My heating engineer looked at the list left by the inspector of the pump and laughed. 'This is what they do,' he said, 'to avoid having to honour their warranty.' In the list of plumbing wrongdoing, he pointed out a number of things that he said made no difference to the functioning of the pump which, amongst other iniquities should, according to the man who inspected the installation, have been connected to the shower thermostat valve by a 22 millimetre pipe. Why did it seem more important than the others? My heating engineer told me that there is no shower thermostat manufactured for domestic use in the UK that has a 22 millimetre connection. The requirement stood out because it was unachievable, a matter which a quick check with the plumbing supply merchant confirmed.

In a week or so, the promised bill arrived in the post. I waited a week or two until I was closer to the payment date they had indicated and wrote a letter to the manufacturer telling them that I had carefully read the report written by their engineer and as he had specified an installation condition which was impossible to meet due to the unavailability of the 22 millimetre connection, their bill was in dispute until I received an explanation. As I write this more than two months later, there has been no explanation and no further request for payment.

As a negotiator, I know that when someone gives you a list of reasons for complying with them, as often happens when they are presenting an argument to you, then you should look for the weakest part of their argument and dispute it. The manufacturer presented me with a condition I could not have complied with – I may have been guilty as charged about the other conditions that included things like pipe length and vent sizes – but their position was fatally undermined by the one weak component.

There are two lessons here for us as negotiators. First, find a good, strong reason to support your argument and stick to it; do not be tempted to cast around for as many reasons as you can muster – they will inevitably get weaker and undermine the strong one. Second, remember my shower connection – put the weakest of others' arguments under pressure and you can threaten all of them.

That said, I am off for a shower!

## Pennies from heaven?
*David Bannister, 10th August 2023*

My tastes in music are very varied but when we sit around the dining table in the evening, my choice is often to listen to the Great American Songbook; a collection of songs and ballads mostly dating back to the 1950s. So, I was very sorry to hear of the recent passing of its greatest exponent, Tony Bennett. Some years ago, I was at a conference in San Francisco and on the final evening, we all had dinner and our host announced 'a special appearance'. We were then entertained to a private cabaret by the great man himself. Believe me, hearing him sing 'I Left My Heart in San Francisco' when the bay is just the other side of the wall is quite something. I have seen him in the UK in concert twice since then and was always captivated by his wonderful voice and demeanour. As some of you reading this may know, he was also a very accomplished artist and some of his paintings hang in illustrious galleries. So, if you are ever stuck for something to get me for my birthday…

Recently, a friend called me and told me that, as a consequence of his employer being bought out, he was facing redundancy. He told me how the matter had been handled and it had not been done well. The recommended procedure had not been followed and, as someone who knows quite a lot about employment law as I have always taken an interest, I helped him to prepare for a meeting to discuss things with his employer. One of the items he proposed was that his employer should finance a consultation with a legal expert in the field. They agreed and he proceeded to discuss their (I thought) derisory offer of severance with the solicitor he selected, with some help from me. He updated me as matters progressed and his solicitor, clearly not one of Scotwork's alumni, haggled the way to a settlement which was significantly, and rightly, a substantial improvement on the original offer from the employer. The deal centred on the financial aspect of the settlement and my friend was very content with the outcome. I bit my tongue when he spoke to me as I thought the lawyer could have introduced more variables to enrich the deal – keep the computer, maintain benefits for a time, be the author of the announcement of his departure and so on. My experience from teaching them on our courses is that lawyers are not the best negotiators; they tend to focus on a financial outcome and can miss opportunities to enhance their deals. My friend, however, was truly happy as his ultimate settlement was very significantly greater than the original basic offer from his employer.

If you are still with me, you have read two apparently entirely unconnected paragraphs and are wondering at exactly what time of day I am writing this and what I may have consumed in the course of my musings. Let me enlighten you. Tony Bennett, artist and crooner, featured in many obituaries and I read a lot of them. He had a career bookended with huge success but in his middle years, before his son took over his management, he abused alcohol and drugs. Helped by his family, he recovered and will be remembered for his wonderful singing and painting. One quote attributed to Bennett is: 'The trick is to survive success. Anyone can survive failure.' I thought about this and it stopped me from discussing anything with my friend other than that he was happy with the successful outcome achieved by his lawyer. Yes, I thought it could have been done differently and could possibly have achieved more but he had decided that he had managed to get what he wanted. Even when further, but less important, concessions may have been possible, he decided that enough was enough. He was content and ready to move on.

It's a lesson for negotiators that being clear about what our objectives are is crucial but also recognising when we have achieved those objectives is critically important too. If you have managed to achieve a settlement providing enough money to buy yourself a new computer, don't push your luck and ask for one on top of what you have already agreed with your counterparty. Wish lists to enrich a deal are essential but the items that comprise them are not to be exhaustively checked off until none are left. Don't hazard success and court potential failure by greedy end-game tactics. Define carefully what success will look like, recognise when you have it and proceed to nail it down so it won't slip through your fingers. Follow in the steps of the great singer and make sure you go (in the words of his song) 'From Rags to Riches' and not the other way around!

# The past is a foreign country: they do things differently there
*Ellis Croft, 21st September 2023*

One crucial way in which skilled negotiators improve the quality of their deal making is by pricing in the different values that parties place on the variables under discussion. Understanding that difference can make the difference between:

- No trade: where we might habitually give something away because we can.
- A poor trade: we place low value on the variable from our perspective, so let it go for too little.
- A good deal: where we price in the extra value the other party places on a variable, even if it's not important to us.

Time can be one of the biggest influencers on differential value. As I embarked on my first full-time job I cannot recall giving the pension benefits that were part of the package a second thought. They were unimportant to me back then. That it was a final salary pension scheme (which may signal how long ago I started my career) only serves to underline the different value that I now place on my pension pot. Recognising that our own values shift is a good start when it comes to appreciating that others place different values on what we trade with.

But we don't need the passage of decades to understand how time and value can be intertwined. As I write this, just over two weeks back from a fortnight away with my family, it's fascinating to reflect on something relatively simple – like how we perceive and appreciate the passage of time. Spent on holiday, it can be luxuriously slow, appreciated in its entirety and prodigious in terms of memorable moments. Contrastingly, on occasion, some of the time spent at work (which I believe the pedants at Greenwich would insist equates to the same value in seconds, minutes and hours) can feel frenetic, even stressful. I suspect most of us would probably agree that in both cases, there's never as much time as we want or need – but possibly from different perspectives. Understanding those perspectives is crucial if we're going to start to be able to gauge what the different values we negotiate with place on common variables – such as time.

If, like many, you price time on holiday with a higher value than time spent at work, that leads us into another major driver of differential value – scarcity. Reversing the balance of time spent at work versus on holiday might create an entirely different perception of value (whatever we might be thinking in the immediate afterglow of a couple of weeks away). Sometimes an offer can be valued so little by its target audience that it is no longer viable – famously Concord announced its final flight just under 20 years ago, in no small part due to declining demand. The last flights available were snapped up in seconds as priceless mementoes.

I'm not suggesting that differential value is always as dramatic – or indeed as obvious – as was the case with Concord. But recognising that the value you place on something may differ – sometimes by a distance – from those you negotiate with will help you strike better deals at any time. Always be curious as to how your opposite party might value variables. Perhaps ask why it might be important – you never know what you might discover.

# Creativity: it's more than just chickens confronting existence

*Ann Parr, 15th August 2024*

As I wandered around Edinburgh this weekend enjoying the atmosphere and sights of the start of the annual Edinburgh Festival Fringe, creativity, like love in the Wet Wet Wet song, was all around. Not just in the creative (OK, frankly sometimes downright bonkers) names of fringe shows: 'Three Chickens Confront Existence' or 'Mitzi Fitz's Glitzy Bitz'; don't ask or indeed even try to say that after a couple of sweet sherries!

There was the street art where a perfectly ordinary pavement in the hands of a skilful artist looked for all the world like one wrong step and it was down into Dante's inferno for the hapless mis-stepper.

'Ah, those crazy creative types,' I mused to myself as I walked past a 20-foot Tin Man from the *Wizard of Oz*. But, if this is art, and negotiation is an art – or a very clever formula that could result in the perfect deal for every negotiator every time – maybe we have more in common with those arty folks than it might at first appear.

Creativity and a creative mindset are crucial skills for a negotiator. Not just a nice to have or, 'If I've got a bit of spare time, I might work on some extra fluffy bits of value to ask the other side for.' No. Crucial. As crucial, I'd wager, as some very sturdy stilts and lots of balance practice to the 20-foot Tin Man.

Creativity is so important to a negotiator because just like an artist knowing what brushes to use to create the effect they want, the mental creativity to think beyond the current circumstances and bring agility of thought and the right skill to the table can make all the difference. Creativity can help the negotiator break out of deadlock, bring value to the other side that can make the impossible suddenly much more likely or turn an already good deal into an even better one.

We talk about the importance of having a wish list at Scotwork and I sometimes think the phrase, to some, may suggest small stuff, fluffy stuff, and almost trivialise the importance of taking time to build a list of creative variables that add value for us or them. A skilfully executed list of creative variables in a well-thought-through wish and concession list can often help the other party see sufficient value for them that they may be able to give us movement where we want it, and that 'small stuff', well, that can put an extra turn on a deal at the end to give us a bit of extra value and a better deal as a result.

A creative mindset and a well-thought-out list of variables can be a game changer for a negotiator.

Now, I'm off to see if there are any tickets left for *Of Mike and Men*... don't ask but apparently it's hilarious!

## Red, red line
*Ellis Croft, 26th September 2024*

I was struck by the language reported this week in coverage of Boeing's negotiations with their workers (or unions, depending on whose point of view you're taking – the employer maintains they're going by the book, the union accuses the proposal of being made via media channels).

The striking phrase – one that we've likely all heard before, and perhaps even used ourselves – was that Boeing's offer was 'best and final'. There's something of a spectrum here in terms of what that might mean. At one end, Boeing have reached the limits to which they are prepared to flex and are entirely comfortable with managing the deadlock that might arise from failing to gain an agreement. At the other end, we have perhaps the more typically seen context in which such language might be used – in a competitive negotiation where one party is trying to robustly manage expectations, but there may still be flexibility to explore in order to gain agreement. In other words, neither 'best' nor 'final'. In either case, my advice would be to think very carefully before asserting a position so absolutely.

Why? Because at either end of the spectrum there is risk. If you have genuinely reached your limit position(s) then signalling that precise information to your counterparty with a 'final' offer might not be in your best interests, particularly if you will be negotiating with them again in the future. Similarly, most of us resent being told 'take it or leave it' and this rarely helps the levels of tension in the negotiation. If, on the other hand, there is flexibility but one party has made the assertion competitively or out of frustration, then the probability will be that further necessary movement exposes the 'final' offer as being, well, not final at all. Not only does this damage the credibility of the party making the 'final' offer, but it may also encourage the counterparty to press even harder. At both ends of the spectrum, there is also the metaphorical trap of painting oneself into a corner, which is rarely a good look.

There are lots of ways in which negotiators can manage these risks. Examples of some are:

- If you are tempted to make a 'final' offer then revisit your preparation and look at where you may be able to trade value outside of the issues that are contentious or at their limits.
- Explore the circumstances in which your counterparty is prepared to be flexible in areas that may offer the opportunity to work towards a workable deal.
- Be prepared to give in areas of lesser importance to secure the agreement you want or need in a more important area.
- Highlight where you may be able to be flexible in order to get what you want.

If in receipt of a 'final' offer then first and foremost probe – ask good questions and understand whether you're dealing with a limit position or simply competitive expectation management. If it's a genuine limit position then explore any other areas where you may still be able to trade value to make the deal implementable at your end (assuming you can live with the limit position, of course). Where it's clearly not a 'final' position then initially don't allow it to influence your view of what a good deal looks like and avoid the temptation to up the stakes in terms of adversarial behaviour (by pointing it out, mirroring it, etc.). Instead, think about how you can help your counterparty move to where they need to with some kind of dignity intact – they're much more likely to offer up flexibility to secure a deal if they feel encouraged and safe to do so.

The 'best and final' offer was made on Monday. On Tuesday, the unions registered their response: 'Not interested.'

# Beware the perils of giving in
*Andy Archibald, 15th February 2024*

The other night I was watching a popular TV programme in the UK called *Dragon's Den*. The show features entrepreneurs pitching their business ideas to the Dragons, multimillionaire investors who decide whether to invest in exchange for a stake in the company.

During this particular episode, two jewellery entrepreneurs asked the Dragons for a £250,000 investment in their business, in exchange for a 3% stake. Two Dragons refused, one agreed, and two demanded a 5% stake. One of the Dragons who demanded 5% was Steven Bartlett, a British entrepreneur, investor and podcaster.

However, to the surprise of the Dragons, the entrepreneurs declined all the proposals and made it clear they were prepared to walk away with nothing. The Dragons were puzzled and asked why they would do such a thing when at least one proposal met their needs. The entrepreneurs explained that they had a preferred Dragon, Steven Bartlett, but that the demand of 5% was beyond their limit (or so the assumption is). The entrepreneurs asked Steven to reconsider, and he took a brief timeout to consider it and consult his notes.

As a negotiation skills trainer, at this point, I assumed (and hoped) he was consulting a list of variables that he could use to trade the 2% concession demanded by the entrepreneurs. Unfortunately, when he responded, it was effectively, 'OK, no problem', giving in to the demand and missing the opportunity to get something in return for the concession. He could have proposed a lower investment in exchange for the concession or staggered the investment over a longer period. By not doing so, he missed a chance to add more value from his point of view. (It's possible, and I hope it's the case, that there was a further negotiation once the cameras stopped rolling.)

Additionally, the response has the danger of setting a precedent for the future. The entrepreneurs saw that he gave in quickly when they said no, which may lead them to take the same approach in future negotiations.

Therefore, it's crucial to have a list of variables to trade when making concessions in negotiations, particularly in long-term relationships where there will be many negotiations to come. Furthermore, avoid setting a precedent by giving in to demands without getting something in return – if it's a demand you can agree to, always trade value in return.

# From left field
*David Bannister, 8th August 2024*

Some time ago, a friend was describing to me the last stages of a somewhat acrimonious divorce. He was telling me how difficult it had been to reach a financial settlement for him and how it was not made easier by the process of both parties negotiating through their solicitors, whose approach seemed rigid. He described how the financial settlement between the parties had reached the point of agreement on the sums involved but that he would have to wait months for his settlement as the 'other side' – as he described it – needed to crystallise some assets and could not do so without penalty for some time. This created some problems for my friend. I suggested that he might offer to accept the delay provided that he could share in some of the bounty the other side would achieve by delaying. He suggested this to his solicitor who said that he could not charge interest – so, said I, call it something else – the name doesn't matter provided that you get the outcome you want! It's a pretty classic, 'If you… then I'.

On a related topic, I am a very long-term fan of Manchester United football club. Recent years have tried the patience of fans – me included – but with the new ownership, hope is returning (or is it blind faith?). A couple of transfer deals at the club have recently caught my eye. The first one is for a United player, Mason Greenwood, who in 2022 was charged with a number of offences against a woman but the charges were dropped after a few months, although he did not appear for the club again. He is a very good player and was on loan for a period last year. The club have just concluded a deal to sell him to Marseille for £26.6m. In the crazy telephone numbers world of football transfers, this player is cheap – many would argue that his market value, free from the taint of allegations about his behaviour, could be twice that figure. But if you look at the smaller print, Manchester United have rid themselves of an expensive problem – they were still paying his astronomical wages until his contract ended – but they have wrapped into the deal that if his new club sell him on during the course of his new contract, United get 50% of any future fee. They have cleverly rid themselves of a problem and it is very unlikely that he would have played again for them, but Marseille, who have bought a good player cheaply have to indemnify United if Greenwood performs well and other wealthy clubs come shopping for him in the future.

While all of this was going on, United acquired two new players – forward Joshua Zirkzee for £36.5m and defender Lenny Yoro for £52m. In Zirkzee's case, United have a clause in the five-year contract to extend the deal for a further year if they wish to do so. In the case of Yoro, the team he is leaving get £52m – a healthy profit – but also have provision in the contract which will push the fee up to £60m if the player meets certain unspecified targets (usually related to winning competitions).

In the world of football these are called 'add-ons' – enhancements to make the deal more acceptable, but on conditions. Like my divorcing friend, these add-ons can be what pushes a deal from being marginal to being acceptable. They are all conditional, involving one party doing something the other party wants and they are not immediate – a carrot rather than a stick if you like. So, when you next do a deal think about the potential for add-ons – enrichment for the future, which makes the deal in the here and now that bit more acceptable.

## The bank is closed...
*Siobhan Bermingham, 3rd October 2024*

A few years ago, in a previous role, I was brought in to do some consultancy work with a company that was attempting to build long-term relationships with well-established firms in their market. They'd been doing several deals over the few years prior but always felt that they weren't getting lucrative deals or developing their relationships. It was evident that they hadn't attended a Scotwork negotiation training course!

As I reviewed their previous deals, they were littered with, dare I say it, 'goodwill gestures'. Free concessions that they'd been shovelling out to these large firms in the belief that these goodwill gestures would build up a bank of 'favour' or 'credit' towards them. Reviewing the deals, it felt as if these larger, more established firms had opened a big bag and swept up unbelievable volumes of free concessions. However, when this company attempted to extract from that 'goodwill bank', the bank was firmly closed or there seemed to be no funds of goodwill coming from the other party. So how could they turn it around after establishing this dynamic over a long period of time?

During internal meetings, I heard the team argue how these goodwill gestures 'hadn't really cost them anything'. I was told repeatedly that they were 'free items/data anyway' and the repeated question, 'What else were we expected to do?'.

We had to take the time to talk about how valuable all these goodwill gestures were to the other party. It took a while to shift the mindset. It's not about how easy it is to give, but how valuable it is to the other party. We explored how they might have traded that value for something they valued in return. Linking conditions with the concessions would have enabled them to get tangible value from the agreements and taught the other party to trade with them and take them seriously as negotiators. It was an uncomfortable but ultimately rewarding change. Soon many more doors were being opened and the 'goodwill bank' became a distant memory for all. They started bargaining and trading value, always keeping in mind the question, 'How valuable is this to the other party?'.

## CHAPTER 7

# CLOSE TO GETTING THE DEAL OVER THE LINE

You've done all the hard work and both parties have almost reached a point where a deal can be struck. At or towards the end of the negotiation there is often an opportunity to draw out issues that have not been finalised, which can provide an opportunity for 'trial closing'. For example, if the other party brings hidden or unresolved issues to the table, you ask the question, 'Are you saying that if I agree to those items, you will be satisfied with the whole deal?'.

Similarly, if there is a question about a minor aspect of your proposal, rather than saying 'yes' or 'no', your answer is that if the other party agrees to the overall proposal you are prepared to concede on these (specific and minor) points.

There can be a tendency here to get greedy; you don't want to snatch a dispute from the jaws of a compromise by being too competitive, so resist the impulse to do so.

## Beware the trap of just one more thing
*Andy Archibald, 12th October 2023*

We've just finished watching the first season of *Poker Face*. For those who haven't watched it, the main character has an almost superhuman ability to tell 100% of the time when someone is lying. I bet many of us wish we had this when we suspect someone is lying to us!

The main character, played brilliantly by Natasha Lyonne, reminds me a lot of the character Columbo, played by the equally brilliant Peter Falk in a show I watched as a kid in the early 1990s. Columbo's famous catchphrase was '… just one more thing', which the character would deliver to crack the case wide open at the precise moment the antagonist in the episode felt they had got away with the crime.

I was also thinking about the Columbo character not long ago. I was delivering a training programme to a client and we were discussing the latter stages of negotiations, where some last-minute demands might need to be managed. In many negotiations, negotiators will effectively try a Columbo and ask for one more thing before they agree to the deal. And if they get it, they might even be tempted to keep asking for more, which can become very costly to the other side.

Therefore, it's vital to keep trading concessions right to the very end and avoid giving things away for free.

I asked the group if they had examples they could share and one did.

They explained they were working as a broker in rare artefacts at the time and were negotiating the sale of an extremely rare fossil for nearly half a million dollars. The negotiation went back and forward, with various concessions made on both sides, and it felt like it was nearing the end of the process and a deal was close. And in any negotiation, when a deal is close, nervousness about losing it might creep in – a lot of work has probably gone into it and we can imagine what it will mean to finally land it, and therefore the result can often be last-minute demands that are given away for free.

In the case of my participant, the last-minute demand they received was for delivery charges to be covered by the broker. The response? 'No problem.'

Deal done.

But later on, while writing up the agreement, my client realised the problem – they didn't know the cost of delivering such a rare artefact. And unfortunately, it's not as simple as booking a delivery with DHL. In fact, it's such a specialist requirement that the cost in this case was £150k, which was a very big concession to make right at the end of the process.

I asked what happened next. 'Luckily, the deal fell through for other reasons,' my client explained.

They got away with it that time, but there's a crucial lesson here. When a deal is close, we are more likely to give away things without considering the value and without making sure we get something in return.

My advice? Keep trading demands right to the very end (even if it's the deal itself as a condition for agreeing to a small, acceptable late demand), know the value of your concessions and keep any last-minute concessions small.

## Do I or don't I say?
### Andy Archibald, 10th November 2022

Earlier this year, we asked the Scotwork Alumni and blog readers to respond to negotiating dilemmas involving controversial situations. We were interested in decisions made with an ethical dimension, which we all must make from time to time during a negotiation.

One of those situations is where the other side makes a mistake but doesn't realise it. And that mistake may have a significant commercial benefit to you but will be detrimental to them.

That poses a dilemma to you as a negotiator. Do you tell the other side, potentially weakening the deal from your point of view but strengthening the relationship? Or do you keep quiet, taking the approach of why interrupt them when they are making mistakes?

I encountered this scenario in my previous role managing commercial partnership contracts and had to decide whether or not to tell the other side about a mistake they had made. In my situation, one of our largest suppliers was due to renew a high-value and long-term contract with us, and I was responsible for managing it and the relationship overall. We had negotiated a deal that satisfied both sides, and the lawyers were drafting the contract.

But while preparing for an internal presentation on the new contract, I noticed the supplier had made an error in one of their figures. The error favoured us quite significantly commercially, and I felt there was a good chance they would sign the contract without realising. But I knew they would eventually notice. And when they did, and we had the inevitable renegotiation, things could turn ugly as both sides might play the blame game, and the whole thing would cost time and money to fix.

After considering the options, I decided we should tell them, even if it was to the dismay of my boss at the time. Because ultimately, it came down to two things. Firstly, it was counterproductive to sign a contract knowing it would need to be renegotiated soon. And secondly, I was the one that had to manage it for another five years (and potentially another five years after that!).

So, what advice is there if or when you encounter this dilemma? The first thing is to ask yourself what the relationship means to you. If it is a one-off transaction and you might never speak to the other side again, then why say anything? But if it is a long-term relationship or contract that requires collaborative working and trust, and there will be future negotiations, it is worthwhile telling them when they have made a mistake.

And if you can, take control of the outcome by making a proposal that corrects the error and suits you more than them; if you highlight the error but leave it open for them to propose the remedy, it is very likely to suit their objectives, not yours.

## CHAPTER 8

# AGREE AND DOCUMENT WHAT HAS BEEN AGREED

It is important to agree what has been agreed, whereby you ensure there are no ambiguities, the actions for implementation are agreed, the agreement is confirmed and documented and they are willing to put it in place. Many deals turn sour as insufficient attention has not been paid to how the deal will be implemented.

### What did I just agree to, again?
*Ellis Croft, 29th February 2024*

One area of negotiation that can end up being frequently overlooked is agreement. In other words, the specific terms and conditions parties are binding themselves to in the contract that the negotiation will produce. For some (including for many years, me) this can be challenging – after all, if the main issues have been traded around to the point that parties are comfortable then agreement must naturally follow. Right?

Well, not quite. Sometimes this can stem from a misunderstanding around the specifics of a particular issue and failing to address them individually during negotiations. I once negotiated a six-figure deal with a supplier (which was substantial for my part of the business), part of which involved some of their employees needing to travel to offices in the US and Asia to fulfil their obligations under the terms of the deal. I agreed that as the customer we would cover their travel costs – it's not exactly unusual to do so. What I didn't do was to agree on precisely what that would involve with regard to costs. No budget, no cap to cover uncertainty, no policy, just a breezy 'yes' to travel costs. Imagine my surprise, therefore, when presented with a chunky five-figure invoice for flights and hotels when I'd been expecting between a quarter and a third (tops!) of that amount. On the one hand, that's entirely on me for my failure to be specific – in that sense, I got exactly what I deserved. On the other hand, the supplier missed the opportunity to ask during the negotiation whether their own travel policies were consistent with ours in relation to the convention of the client covering supplier travel costs. Had either of us focussed fully on the agreement we would have had the chance to establish whether we could have resolved a situation we'd all rather have avoided, in advance. I did resolve the situation, but it was costly and the important point was that I should not have allowed it to happen in the manner it did in the first place.

Issues that may, in the context of the deal itself, appear relatively small can become contentious later in this manner. An abstract or concept – who holds stock – might be easy to agree based on assumption. But it's important not to let the closure of the deal get in the way of clarifying issues, however relatively small they may appear at the time. If it's stock – how much? For how long? Who'll cover the costs of delivery, insurance and other ancillary, but necessary, expenses? And so on. It's far better to discover your assumptions need revisiting when you're still working with a live deal than when the contract has been signed. At best, you may be able to trade greater value in the overall deal from understanding exactly what you're agreeing to, where it's important to the other party. You'll also avoid the pernicious and almost unavoidable suspicion that the other party may have deliberately taken advantage of your assumption, if they didn't raise the issue themselves at the time – and that will preserve the ongoing relationship. And, at the very least, you'll avoid ending up with egg on your face.

Our advice? It's simple – agree what you've agreed. And while that sounds almost laughably easy, you don't have to scratch the surface of too many deals to see where agreement is relative or subjective, and potentially therefore not as mutual as we may believe.

## Mine all mine

*Tom Feinson, 4th April 2024*

In 1994, as part of the privatisation of the coal industry, the UK government committed to protecting mineworkers' pensions. In return (kudos to the government), as part of the agreement, the government was to get 50% of any surplus to the scheme. On the face of it, this sounds like a pretty sensible contingency agreement, sometimes described as the trading of opinions. I assume, based on the agreement, that the unions stated an opinion that the pension fund would not be able to meet obligations, whilst the government took an opposing point of view. If so, both parties attempting to predict the outcome of a future event represents an argument of opinion that could go on for some time. Better to construct an agreement that recognises the other party's inhibition and rewards your opinion if you are subsequently proved right.

Tangentially, it's also worth recognising risk as a key value driver. People tell us that it's all about the money but in truth, for most of us, risk mitigation is as – if not more – important. This agreement demonstrates that the union were, at the time, prepared to give up the potential for more money in return for financial security.

Back to the point. Thirty years later there is a problem: one party is very unhappy with the agreement and the other, frankly, delighted. In July 2023, the Business, Economic and Industry Strategy committee (BEIS) concluded that participation in the pension scheme had dramatically reduced since 1994, for obvious reasons, which had substantially reduced government risk. However, the price for taking that risk had not been recalibrated accordingly. The BEIS committee recommended a review of the scheme and the sharing arrangements. The government had made £4.4bn since the introduction of the scheme.

The unions argue that the government have a moral obligation to the change the terms of the agreement and that they should not benefit off the backs of miners and their widows. Returning the money would see an increase of £14 per week to the average pension of £84 per week.

The government, on the other hand, are of the view that an agreement is an agreement and both parties freely entered into it and have benefitted from it. A BEIS spokesperson says, 'Mineworkers' pension scheme members are receiving payments 33% higher than they would have been thanks to the government's guarantee and scheme members have received bonuses in addition to their guaranteed pension.'

The unions are saying that, whilst this may have been a sensible arrangement 20 years ago, it isn't now. Is it even true? Interestingly the pension trustees, when offered, preferred to keep the existing arrangement rather than lose the guarantee in return for keeping all the surplus. If the desire is to get the money and keep the guarantee then it's doomed to fail. You can't have your cake and eat it.

One lesson to draw from this is to build parameters for change into contingency contracts, recognising that they should be balanced to benefit both parties.

The broader question is whether there is a moral obligation on a party to renegotiate the terms of an agreement that they are not contractually obliged to simply because circumstances have rendered it unfavourable to the other party.

Classically, the answer would be that people and organisations must be motivated to negotiate; they need to see it as being in their interest.

What's your take? I'd love to hear your perspective.

## When you let 'the boss' get involved in the negotiation when they are not prepared

*John McMillan, 21st March 2024*

This story is from 2021 from the Politico political website when Boris Johnston was the UK Prime Minister; he got involved in a negotiation which was not his remit. Ever keen to show that Brexit benefits were more than just being able to buy our vegetables in stones, pounds and ounces, he was hosting a dinner at No. 10 for the Australian Prime Minister Scott Morrison and made an unplanned concession with huge ramifications for British beef farmers.

One might assume that drink was taken. Boris told the Prime Minister that he would agree to Australian beef imports being measured by weight of the cut meat rather than the (heavier) full carcass. This was a major concession that had not been agreed by the negotiators, or by the International Trade Secretary, Liz Truss.

According to Adam Frost's report in *The Independent*, 'Australian high commissioner, George Brandis, scrawled down the unexpected bonus on a napkin and fled to the loo.' On the way he gave it to an aide to scan and turn into a trade document – before it was returned to the dinner for Mr Johnson to sign; which he did.

Ms Truss was said to have been 'livid' when she learned of Mr Johnson's concession over breakfast the following morning. 'Your boss has already conceded the whole kingdom,' Australia's chief negotiator Dan Tehan told her, according to a former minister involved in the talks.

Brexit negotiator David Frost was at the dinner with Mr Johnson and Mr Morrison. One former Truss adviser said, 'Frost was over the detail, but I don't think Boris was,' adding that the dinner 'was very slapdash – and ultimately ended up giving more on beef.'

Advisers said Ms Truss wanted the talks reopened after Mr Johnson's concession – but Mr Morrison threatened to 'tell the media the UK was going back on its first post-Brexit trade deal.'

A spokesperson for the NFU (National Farmers' Union) added: 'We know the government gave away much more than they needed to, and this illustrates it.'

This illustrates two negotiating principles:

1. Don't let the boss near the negotiation unless they are fully briefed and are effective negotiators.
2. If you win an unexpected concession, summarise it, and record it as soon as possible; agree what is agreed.

# Wanna bet?

*Ellis Croft, 13th June 2024*

News that one of Rishi Sunak's aides allegedly placed a wager on the date of the general election mere days before it was announced is causing ripples in the already turbulent waters of the current news cycle. Of course, we must acknowledge – rightly – the presumption of innocence in this and all such cases, as a matter of principle. However, on the basis that Rishi Sunak was unlikely to have sprung the news of his decision on his inner circle out of the blue (it's hard to imagine he told the cabinet and his aides at No. 10 on the day he made his announcement, 'just popping out for a pint of milk, be right back', for example), the 'routine inquiries' faced by the aide in question are likely to be uncomfortable for him, if not downright awkward.

People bet for all sorts of reasons – and they can be a very useful option open to negotiators as well. Many negotiations feature important variables that intrinsically depend on future conditions that are uncertain – how will supply chain pressures affect key variables such as delivery dates or component pricing? What will a potential change of government in the world's largest economy do to the market for renewable energy? Is the tapering off of inflation a long-term trend we can incorporate into multi-year contracts or will it return? So much of what we trade can be affected by the uncertainty around events that are yet to happen – and this frequently results in a good deal of arguments between parties in conflict over those variables. These are arguments that most often take time and lead nowhere. For example, a supplier asserting that inflation will still be higher in their industry well into next year so the headline rate is irrelevant, is unlikely to change their mind on that any more than the buyer will be likely to acquiesce to evidence to the contrary. Firstly, we simply don't know yet. Secondly – and crucially – if it's not in my interests to concede an argument about what's yet to happen, why would I?

Where agreeing to disagree and postponing the conflict is possible, that may be for the best. Frequently that isn't possible

– and that's where a well-constructed bet may be very useful for negotiators. The ability to cut through the disagreement with a trade that rewards the party who is correct can enable negotiators to move forward towards a deal rather than being stuck in an endless circular argument in which nobody will yield.

Not only can a bet move the process forward. It is also a very useful tool to identify where an argument is simply being made to reinforce a position, rather than because it's a genuinely held belief. There will be times when parties in conflict put forward a position simply because it suits them and if they can persuade you they are right, you are more likely to concede ground. Placing a bet that would reward them if their views turned out to be accurate will test the authenticity of the argument. Back in 2006, Arsenal – my team – faced Barcelona in the European Cup final in Paris. Exchanging opinions with a Barça supporting friend, who was looking forward to watching the favourites thrash Arsenal, I naturally offered a contrary view, maintaining that Arsenal would be a revelation as we had a world-class striker in Thierry Henry, and more. This conversation went round and round until my friend offered me a £50 bet on the outcome. At which point my confidence evaporated and I backpedalled as fast as I could – it was not a genuinely held opinion and I didn't particularly want to lose out on £50. We came close – not close enough, though. But at least I didn't lose £50 to boot. Trading opinion can be a very useful tool in the negotiating skillset – it's always worth looking for the opportunity to do so, particularly where you sense the contrary view is a tactical play.

## Agreeing: the work of the devil
*Ellis Croft, 5th October 2023*

Back in the 1990s, when I'd been sent by my employers to learn about how to negotiate more effectively, I recall thinking about the final two steps (**Close** and **Agree**) – well really, what's the substantive difference? Any deal not aligned with both parties' interests (i.e. agreed) surely can't be closed? And if you're closing a deal – well, how can you do *that* if there's disagreement about the variables on the table?

Over the next 25 years, I set about experiencing the sometimes painful differences between two distinct – and very important – stages in negotiating! And a couple of recent events have really made me think about how we can illustrate the critical differences. Firstly, let's head to Washington DC where the US government narrowly avoided shutdown through gaining agreement on budget funding, albeit for the not-very-reassuring period of 45 days. As reported, the price that Joe Biden paid to veer away from the cliff edge was the removal of funding for Ukraine's defence over that time period. That closed the deal. So it must be agreed, right? Maybe not – let's see what Biden said in the immediate aftermath of the 'agreement': 'We cannot, under any circumstances, allow US support to Ukraine to be interrupted.' If I was going to characterise that statement in relation to the budget deal, 'disagreement' might be the word that springs to mind. The obvious problem with a fundamental disagreement in our day-to-day negotiations is that implementation of the deal may become problematic – and we'll see how this plays out in the US between now and the next deadline.

Whatever happens, I doubt folk will look upon last week's deal and think of it as being an agreement, despite the deal being struck.

But our ability to agree isn't only impacted by opposing differences in philosophy or opinion. Sometimes it can be very basic. In North London at the weekend, with a player already sent off, Liverpool broke up the field and surprised Tottenham Hotspur by scoring. Or so they thought – until the goal was flagged offside. But! The introduction of the Video Assistant Referee (VAR) in football has enabled an absolute decision – such as offside – to be clarified through the use of technology. The fact that Liverpool's Diaz looked fairly obviously onside to me (and just about everyone watching) made the VAR decision to uphold the offside flag all the more baffling. How did that happen? The audio recording of the 'process' reveals the truth – and it's hilarious/appalling depending on your point of view. The officials making the decision assumed they were confirming an awarded goal, not a disallowed one – making it a 'perfect call' in the (possibly last, at least in a VAR context) words of the official concerned. Sometimes agreement can fall apart for entirely absurd reasons – meaning every negotiator should be conscious about being very clear when they make deals.

So, agreeing a deal – it's not always as easy as it might sound. Some advice – be clear, hunt down and eliminate ambiguity, and where substantial differences of opinion may exist, allocate appropriate time to focus on the implementation of the deal. The devil, after all, is in the detail.

# ONCE UPON A DEAL...
# – AUTHOR BIOS

## John McMillan (Scotwork Founder)

I started negotiating when I ran the university student publications department and later in my job as a sales engineer. Nobody taught me what to do as there was no training available.

In 1975, when I set up Scotwork, intending to do something completely different, I recognised this was a need in the market that was not being addressed. Using my personal experience and some insights of others, I created our flagship course, now called Advancing Negotiating Skills.

The four things I enjoy the most are: (1) crafting a deal where the value is greater than the sum of the parts; (2) trading opinions where being correct pays off; (3) meeting someone years later who says, 'It was the best course I ever attended'; and finally, (4) walking away from the deal. This last one is so much fun that I almost will the other side to give me a reason to walk. This conditions my thought process throughout the negotiation and removes any fear of the counterparty's sanction threats.

## Alan Smith

I've spent the last 40 years of my commercial career dealing with 'misaligned objectives' between parties. The trouble is, most people think that the misalignment has been caused by an inability to persuade the other side(s) of the validity and quality of their position.

Since joining Scotwork as a negotiation consultant almost 17 years ago, the prism through which I view such differences has changed. Of course, if I recognise that I may be able to convince you to see things my way I'll stop there. But if I can find a different solution that recognises your needs and delivers them in a way that creates a better outcome for me, it is easier to come to an agreement that cements our relationship.

## Stephen White

Trained as a lawyer, with experience in big-company sales and marketing, I realised early in my career that negotiating expertise did not come easily to most people. There were many books and theories but not much to help negotiators pragmatically in their working environment. Teaching the Scotwork course revealed to me that well-told stories about real negotiations resonated with our audiences more than anything else. This book contains some of those stories.

## Horace McDonald

Before joining Scotwork, I worked in sales, general management and leadership roles in FMCG and the music industry and encountered vastly different styles and approaches. The best thing about being an expert in negotiation is when someone asks me what I do for a living (you'd be surprised how many people don't know negotiation training is available) and their look of wonder when I give them my top three negotiation tips.

## David Bannister

My long fascination with negotiating began when, as a young industrial relations officer, I sat in smoky rooms with union representatives learning the hard way about how tough it can be. Many years later, covering a career that has taken me all over the world and, as a consultant, into many different businesses, I know that when you have negotiating competence at your disposal, you will use these skills to good effect every day.

## Tom Feinson

Born a twin I was introduced to conflict at an early age, causing rather than resolving. It wasn't until many years later that I became involved and fascinated by resolving conflict, you know what they say, 'To catch a thief…'.

My time in negotiation has taken me across continents, included corporate giants as well as disruptor start-ups and straddled both not for profit and commercial sectors. It has always struck me that despite a myriad of contexts, cultures and styles negotiating behaviour is remarkably consistent. The stories in this book reveal the underlying structure to all negotiations and provide simple practical advice on effectively managing the negotiation process.

To give yourself an edge, understand what people are doing not just what they are saying.

## Annabel Shorter

When the lure of a Vauxhall Cavalier proved too powerful, I entered the world of sales. As I moved on the deals got bigger and more complex and the ability to negotiate effectively while building strong relationships became ever more important. I believe our skills and strategies are often a powerful amalgam of everything we have seen, good and bad, from bosses, peers, parents and possibly even reality TV! Examining, questioning and improving can never be a bad thing.

## Ellis Croft

There's an old saying about how to a man with a hammer every problem looks like a nail. And that's how I – and many people, to be fair – used to negotiate. I didn't carry an actual hammer, just in case you were worrying. But I lacked an ability to assess, and options from which to choose in terms of negotiating better deals. A toolkit, even. Learning about the variety that choices give you and making some new mistakes instead of the old ones is fun, a pleasure and a privilege to share through some of the sillier stories I've been part of over the years.

## Ann Parr

For the last 24 years I have spent my working life helping people get more of what they want through the art of negotiation. Following a career in FMCG, which took me around the world, I have been fortunate enough to work at all levels across a vast variety of industries and cultures. Negotiation is an ever-present part of all our lives (both commercial and personal) and I strongly believe developing skills in this area has a hugely positive impact on all our relationships.

## Siobhan Bermingham

As the youngest of six children, I was always competitive and wanted to prove myself. I found that this determination to get the deal done and 'win' had worked well, but not for long. As my commercial career progressed and I negotiated contracts in a range of cultures and industries from digital product distribution, events management, the electric vehicles industry and working with entrepreneurs/start-ups, I knew that I had to develop skills far beyond competitiveness. Becoming more interested in what the other party really wants/needs, having greater flexibility when negotiating and trading based on relative value, certainly helped me shift the size of the deals I was involved in, even when competing against bigger players in my previous industries.

# Index

abuses of power 56–58
achievement of objectives, recognising 156–158
add-ons 168
adjournment 98
adversarial styles 65
aggressive behaviour 56–58
agility 6, 23
Agree step 39, 177–188
AI (Artificial Intelligence) 20–21
alternatives, ensuring 104
ambiguity 89, 123, 177, 187
ambitious proposals 122–123
Archibald, Andy 38–40, 109–112, 165–166, 172–174
Argue step 39, 41–74
articulating your goals 45
assertiveness 58, 131
assumptions, checking 32–33, 71, 83

bad news 45, 64, 150
Bannister, David 2–5, 56–58, 58–61, 76–78, 78–82, 82–85, 101–104, 112–115, 117–119, 137–140, 153–156, 156–158, 166–168
  author bio 191
Bargain step 39, 102, 147–169
'Bargaining Arena' 83
basis of the proposal, probing 8–9
Bermingham, Siobhan 12–14, 20–21, 32–33, 34–36, 98–100, 145–146, 168–169
  author bio 193
'best and final' offer 163
betting 36–38, 183–185

body language/nonverbal communication 76, 78, 91, 127
bosses in negotiations 182–183
breakdown of negotiations 87–89
broad perspectives/overviews 11–12
bullying 56–58, 59, 136

chatbots 20–21
Close step 39, 147, 186–188
cognition 52–53
collaboration
  cooperative stance 6, 51, 58, 65, 98, 129
  female negotiators 131–132
  as negotiation style 50–51, 56, 65–66, 98, 131–132
  relationship-building 6, 50–51, 65–66, 98, 121
common interest 83
communication 57
competitive style 51–52, 64–65, 66, 98, 129
competitor information 26
compliance 112, 155–156
concessions
  art of negotiation 24
  Bargain step 147–148
  concession list 2
conditionality 74, 111–112, 120, 139
differential value 152
'elk steak' 139
goodwill gestures 13–14, 100–101, 146, 169

concessions *(continued)*
 Proposal step 106
 trading variables 165–166
 understanding the other party's value 130
 unexpected 182, 183
conditions
 Bargain step 147–148, 167–168, 169
 concessions 74, 111–112, 120, 139
 Packaging step 138, 139
 Preparation step 13
confirmation bias 19
conflict 49–50, 51, 53, 137, 184–185
consensus 121, 139
consequences for non-compliance 112, 155–156
constructive feedback 59
contingency agreements 180, 181
controversial situations 174–176
cooperation 6, 51, 58, 65, 98, 129
 *see also* collaboration
counterproposals 98, 111, 147–169
creativity 6, 161–162
credibility 7, 80–81, 98, 114–115, 122
criticism, receiving 59
Croft, Ellis 16–18, 18–20, 22–24, 28–30, 46–48, 50–52, 54–55, 64–66, 72–74, 85–87, 90–92, 92–94, 121–123, 123–125, 151–153, 159–161, 177–179, 183–185, 186–188
 author bio 192

data-gathering stages 32–33
deadlocks 115
deal breakers 30, 103, 117
deception 123–125, 126
decision support systems 21
decline, managing 17
defensiveness 60, 61
deferral of action 89, 109
dependency 151
détente 89
differential value 152, 159–161, 169
disagreements 60–61, 85, 186–187
disclosure of information 83
 *see also* information-sharing
discounts 106, 145–146, 149
documentation 177–188
due diligence 32
dynamic pricing 134

'elk steak' 139
emotions 53, 57, 60, 127, 132
errors 174–175
escalations of events 3, 49
ethical dilemmas 174–176
expectations management 19, 114–115, 146, 163
extreme proposals 108, 149–150

face, loss of 4, 33, 114
facts, reliance on 7, 32–33, 125–128
false information 123–125
Feinson, Tom 42–43, 48–50, 106–109, 143–145, 148–151, 179–182
 author bio 191
female negotiators 130–132, 136–137
'final' offers 162–164
first, going 117–119
flashiness 94–96
flexibility
 Bargain step 163, 164
 objectives 6
 Packaging step 131

Preparation step 23, 26, 30
Proposal step 117
Signals step 75, 76, 86
forecasts 18–20
free concessions (goodwill gestures) 13–14, 100–101, 146, 169

gambling/betting 36–38, 183–185
gender stereotypes 130–132, 136
gestures/nonverbal communication 76, 78, 91, 127
goal alignment 56
goal articulation 45
going first 117–119
good questions 19, 39, 42, 53, 71–72, 99–100, 111
goodwill gestures 13–14, 100–101, 146, 169
greed 158
guarantees 54–55, 88–89, 102–103, 153–154, 181

haggling 108, 143
'hidden' issues 139, 171
hostility, coming up against 27–28
hyperbole 67–68

impasses 115
imprecision 123–125
information-gathering 39
information-sharing 45, 65–66, 67–68, 83–85
inhibitions 129, 180
instinct 45
intends 1, 30, 134
interests, identifying 129

Judo 130

kicking the can down the road 89, 109

lack of reaction 84
last-minute demands 173
leverage 3–4, 18, 72–74, 100, 103–104
lies 123–125, 126, 127
limit positions 163, 164
listening, effective 42, 47, 53, 55, 78
long-term relationships 6, 100, 166, 168
'loss aversion' bias 150
loss of face 4, 33, 114
loyalty, rewarding 34
luck 68–70

machismo 113, 114, 136
'make me an offer' 90–91
managing expectations 19, 114–115, 146, 163
McDonald, Horace 6–12, 14–16, 24–27, 30–32, 36–38, 43–46, 61–64, 70–72, 115–117, 133–135, 135–137
author bio 190–191
McMillan, John 182–183
author bio 189
message transmission 17
mind control 90–92
mindset reframes 43
misinformation 123–125, 126, 127
mistakes/errors 174–175
misunderstandings 60, 61, 178
must-haves 1, 30, 31
mutual satisfaction 64–65, 99–100

'niceness' 131
'no' 39–40
non-negotiables 1, 30, 31
nonverbal communication 78, 91, 127

objectives
  focus on 6
  not the same as strategy 1
  Preparation step 23, 24, 26
  prioritisation 103
  recognition of objectives' success 158
  revealing 45
  understanding the other parties' 47, 48
obstacles, awareness of 28–30
off-track, going 141
opening statements 42, 45, 117, 149–150
openness 43–46, 50–51, 65
opinions, trading of 180, 185
opposition, overcoming 23
optimism 70
other-party's eyes, seeing with 2, 18, 48
overviews/broad perspectives 11–12

Package step 35, 39, 129–146
Parr, Ann 5–6, 130–132, 161–162
  author bio 192–193
partners (on your own team), working with 141–142
partnership working (with opposing teams) 6, 120–121
perspectives, taking the other party's 2, 18, 47–48
persuasion 46–48, 67–68, 116–117
pitching first 117–119
posture 76, 78
power balance
  Argue step 56, 72–74
  judging 3–4
  leverage 3–4, 18, 72–74, 100, 103–104
  powerlessness 56, 111
  Proposal step 100, 120
  responding to signals 92–94

precedent 4, 80, 138, 146, 166
predictions 11–12, 18–20
Preparation step 1–40, 132
price increases 149
pricing 133–135, 144–145, 149, 152–153
principles 144, 145
prioritisation of objectives 103
probability-based predictions 20
problem-solving approaches 47, 92, 93, 129
procrastination 127
Proposal step 39, 97–128, 137, 147
push-back 150, 151

questions, effective 19, 39, 42, 53, 71–72, 99–100, 111

realistic proposals 103, 111, 114–115, 122, 127, 137
reciprocity 66, 81
recognition of objectives' success 158
red lines 162–164
reflecting back 78
refusals/rejections 110, 150
relationship-building
  Argue step 41, 45
  collaborative style 6, 50–51, 65–66, 98, 121
  informing other party of an error 175
  long-term relationships 6, 100, 166, 168
  mutually beneficial 99
  rewarding loyalty 34
  with suppliers 35
  trade-offs 174, 175
  *see also* trust
renegotiation 175, 181
resolving all possible issues 139, 171

restrictions 120
  see also conditions
rewarding/punishing signals
  86–87, 93, 107–108
risk 121–123, 151, 180
rogue partners 141–142
'rule of thirds' 149

sanctions 93, 107–108
scarcity 153, 160
second-guessing 19
self-awareness 51
sharing information 45, 65–66,
  67–68, 83–85
shoes, walking in the other's 2,
  18, 48
Shorter, Annabel 27–28
  author bio 192
Signals step 39, 75–96
silence as negotiating tactic 83–85
slogans 46–48
Smith, Alan 52–53, 68–70,
  104–106, 141–143
  author bio 189–190
specificity 178
stakeholders, knowing your 7–8, 32
stereotypes 131, 132
stimulus-response 17
strategy 1, 12, 26
style of negotiation 50–52
  see also collaboration;
    competitive style
success, defining 158
Sumo 130
supplier relations 34–36
'System 2' thinking 52–53

tactics 57, 79, 84–85, 112–115, 150
talent, attracting 10–12
teams of negotiators 141–143,
  182–183
temperature-taking 18

terms and conditions 177–178
thinking processes 52–53
time
  differential value 152–153, 159
  Packaging step 140–141
  Proposal step 115, 127
  Signals step 80, 81
time management 10
  as variable 9, 52–53, 130
time outs 53
tone of conversations 60–61, 76,
  78, 100, 113
trade-offs 148, 174
trading 13, 14, 30, 47, 92, 103
trading of opinions 180, 185
trial closing 171
trust
  Argue step 41, 45, 51, 64, 65
  cooperation 6, 98
  creating a tone of 100
  informing other party of an
    error 175
  Signals step 76
truth 123–125, 126, 127

uncertainty principle 123
unconditional concessions 13, 14,
  74, 120, 138, 139
understanding the other party
  Argue step 47, 48, 53, 61, 71
  checking understanding 78
  good questions 19, 39, 42, 53,
    71–72, 99–100, 111
  Packaging step 131
  Proposal step 99
  Signals step 75–96
unilateral action 16, 88, 89, 121
unknowns 83

value, differential 152, 159–161, 169
value creation outcomes 98
'very British smile' 91

warranties 154–155
   *see also* guarantees
watching for signals 78
'What's in it for me [WIIFM]?'
   92–94
White, Stephen 67–68, 87–89,
   94–96, 117–119, 125–128,
   140–141

author bio 190
win-lose 98
win-win 98
wish lists 2, 14, 139, 158, 162

# A quick word from Practical Inspiration Publishing...

We hope you found this book both practical and inspiring – that's what we aim for with every book we publish.

We publish titles on topics ranging from leadership, entrepreneurship, HR and marketing to self-development and wellbeing.

Find details of all our books at: www.practicalinspiration.com

 **Did you know...**

We can offer discounts on bulk sales of all our titles – ideal if you want to use them for training purposes, corporate giveaways or simply because you feel these ideas deserve to be shared with your network.

We can even produce bespoke versions of our books, for example with your organization's logo and/or a tailored foreword.

To discuss further, contact us on info@practicalinspiration.com.

 **Got an idea for a business book?**

We may be able to help. Find out more about publishing in partnership with us at: bit.ly/PIpublishing.

*Follow us on social media...*

- @PIPTalking
- @pip_talking
- @practicalinspiration
- @piptalking
- Practical Inspiration Publishing